When You Have a Visually Impaired Student with Multiple Disabilities in Your Classroom

A Guide for Teachers

JANE N. ERIN

SUSAN J. SPUNGIN, *Consulting Editor*

PRESS
New York

Printed in the United States of America

Library of Congress Cataloging-in-Publication Data
Erin, Jane N.
   When you have a visually impaired student with multiple disabilities in your classroom : a guide for teachers / Jane N. Erin ; Susan J. Spungin, consulting editor.
      p. cm.
Includes bibliographical references.
   ISBN 0-89128-873-2 (pbk. : alk. paper)
   1. Children with visual disabilities—Education. 2. Children with disabilities—Education. I. Spungin, Susan Jay. II. Title.

HV1638.E75 2004
371.91—dc22

2003024702

The American Foundation for the Blind—the organization to which Helen Keller devoted more than 40 years of her life—is a national nonprofit whose mission is to eliminate the inequities faced by the ten million Americans who are blind or visually impaired.

It is the policy of the American Foundation for the Blind to use in the first printing of its books acid-free paper that meets the ANSI Z39.48 Standard. The infinity symbol that appears above indicates that the paper in this printing meets that standard.

Contents

Buying flowers during an orientation and mobility lesson.

1 Where Do I Begin?

As a special educator, a classroom teacher, or an educational team member, you may be working with a visually impaired student for the first time or as an experienced professional. This booklet provides information on how visual impairment affects learning in communication, movement, self-care skills, and other important areas, and on how to work effectively with students who have visual and other disabilities. It will help you to understand

- how visual impairment affects the ways an exceptional student learns,

- what you can do to help the student understand the environment and learn effectively,

- how you can work comfortably and successfully with a student who is visually impaired and has other disabilities,

- how you can assist other members of the team in understanding the student's visual impairment,

- what types of accommodations and modifications the student may need,

- what additional skills the student may need to learn, and

- where to get additional information and assistance.

DIVERSE NEEDS, DIVERSE ABILITIES

Students with visual and multiple disabilities are diverse in their abilities, interests, ability to use vision and other senses, family background, and personality. Even those who have similar medical conditions may function very differently. Students may have severe retardation or be intellectually gifted; they may be physically limited by cerebral palsy or other physical conditions; they may be very talkative or unable to speak; and they may enjoy hugs and touches or avoid physical contact. (See "Diversity and Variability: Key Concepts" for a discussion of differences among students who have disabilities in addition to visual impairment.)

Family members and caregivers may wonder whether these characteristics result from the child's disabling conditions, learning experiences, or personality, but for most children there is no clear answer to this question. Regardless of the source of such differences among children, your most important goal as a teacher is to create an educational plan that reflects a particular child's individual capabilities and needs. Being flexible and trying to understand how best to work with the child according to his or her strengths are of great help in moving toward that goal. Teachers need both flexibility and information on the impact of vision loss on a student in working to understand that child's capabilities. Many students have complex medical histories, and the extent of the documentation about their medical conditions can sometimes be overwhelming. While it is important to review a student's medical background, keep in mind that medical diagnoses alone do not dictate appropriate instructional strategies. Regular observation and assessment of the child are the most reliable sources of information on his or her educational needs.

Students with visual and multiple disabilities vary widely in visual abilities and their use of vision. Those who have severe visual impairments but are able to use their vision for learning activities are described as having *low vision*, while those who need to use touch and hearing for most learning are considered to be *blind*. Many visually impaired children have a neurological dysfunction, and their lack of a normal visual response may be based on an inability to interpret or notice visual information, rather than on a difference or dysfunction in ocular structures.

2

Diversity and Variability: Key Concepts

Like all children, students with visual and multiple disabilities are individuals. They vary in personalities and preferences, and their disabilities affect them in different ways. The terms used to describe people with disabilities that occur together may also vary. When some professionals or programs describe a child as *multiply disabled*, they mean that he or she has severe and permanent differences in several critical functional areas such as communication and life skills. Others may use the term *multiply disabled* to describe a child who has a visual impairment and one other disabling condition, such as a learning disability that affects reading. The term is so broad and the category so general that it often lacks descriptive value. It is necessary to meet and observe a child to discover individual characteristics and to make decisions about appropriate instruction.

All children, including those with multiple disabilities, vary in such characteristics as

- personality
- motivation
- memory ability
- learning ability
- likes and dislikes
- health
- movement ability
- sensitivity to the environment
- communication form
- expression of feelings
- physical strength
- reasoning

Children with visual and multiple impairments may have a greater range of variation in these areas than other children, and their characteristics are influenced by the quality of the senses and physical capabilities available to them.

Perhaps the visual sensation for children with neurological differences is similar to the disorientation we feel when we awaken after a deep sleep and are aware of light and color but cannot interpret what we see. Children may also have eye conditions that limit the clarity and range of vision, so that their world is blurry or has missing sections. Children who have little or no vision will learn mainly through hearing and touch, and it is especially important for them to have physical contact with learning materials and involvement in events. The teacher of students who are visually impaired can provide information on how much vision a student has and how he or she can use this vision to learn.

Identifying children who have both visual impairments and other disabilities is complex, because states vary in how they define eligibility for services. While federal law broadly defines multiply disabled children as those who have more than one condition that requires adaptation in order to learn, state definitions, which are generally more specific, vary. Many states identify a child with multiple disabilities as one who has limitations in several functional areas, such as communication, adaptive living, and mobility. This child may not be able to read and write, or even to communicate using speech or sign language. Children may also have additional disabilities that are more difficult to evaluate, such as learning disabilities or emotional disorders. These differences may not be identified because family members, teachers, or other professionals attribute differences in academic functioning or behavior to the child's visual impairment.

Students with visual impairment and other disabilities are educated in varying settings. They may be fully or partly included in classrooms with nondisabled students, or they may be educated in a separate classroom. Some students attend specialized schools for blind children or for children with other disabilities. Placement decisions are made after a child's individual needs are identified and an Individualized Education Program (IEP) is developed. Decisions about the appropriate educational setting are influenced by a variety of factors, including family preference, school size and location, the student's individual characteristics, and the school or educational team's philosophies.

THE IMPACT OF VISUAL AND MULTIPLE IMPAIRMENTS ON LEARNING

Vision loss interferes with a child's ability to derive information from the surrounding world. In general, when a visual impairment is combined with other disabilities, the child is further limited in access to information or experiences that are beyond arm's reach. Without an ability to observe objects and events at even a short distance, one's development of concepts about these objects and events is impaired. Visual impairment, therefore, may have a significant impact on a child's cognitive and linguistic development. In addition, an inability to perceive objects typically reduces a child's motivation to move and to explore; this, in turn, can further limit his or her experience and conceptual base. The child may not learn incidentally, through noticing events in the environment, as a seeing child would, or by associating sound, touch, and experience as a blind child who has no other disabilities would. This may mean that he or she has limited experience and, as a result, less-than-complete development of certain concepts. For example, a child who has touched only the family dog and a neighbor's dog may believe that all dogs are large animals with long hair like these two pets. Another child may enjoy the sounds of words but may not use them appropriately or meaningfully, and thus may repeat a favorite phrase from the radio without understanding what it means, or may use *echolalia* (repeated speech) to imitate an angry outburst from a classmate, without being able to describe his or her own emotions or reaction. In some cases, a child who does not have opportunities for interacting with objects and people may substitute repetitive or *stereotypic* behaviors like rocking or biting his or her hands (see Chapter 6).

Children with these types of limitations usually learn best about the world around them when they have a consistent schedule that offers repeated opportunities for sensory experiences. A child who cannot move independently toward objects and places of interest needs to be assisted in moving, or the objects must be moved so that he or she can experience them directly. For example, a learner who hears a vacuum cleaner without seeing or touching it may not understand the size, shape, and purpose of the device, and may be frightened by its noise—or may ignore it after it becomes familiar—if there is not an opportunity to understand the source.

In instances when impaired capacity limits memory span and complex thinking, a child's visual impairment may hinder the generalization of learning over time. He or she may not perceive similarities in repeated experiences like mealtime or play activities if materials, people, and places vary. Visual disability may limit the perception of cues like color or shape that help in understanding distinctive features of a routine. If a child cannot remember that "snack" comes after "play," and cannot see the teacher getting out place mats and cups, the routine may seem new and unpredictable each time it occurs.

For children with visual and multiple disabilities, learning generally must involve gradual expansion from immediate sensory information to skills that involve memory, generalization, and understanding of concepts. For example, a child may be taught to choose between an apple and a cracker by placing the child's right hand on the apple and her left hand on the cracker. Later, the teacher or parent can touch one hand to the apple first, and then the cracker, so that the child will need to remember both items and their locations. If she can progress to the use of abstract symbols, she may later make a choice by signing "apple" when another person signs "You want apple or cracker?" This process will be described in more detail in later sections.

What can be done when a visual impairment that occurs with other disabilities limits a child's ability to generalize learning across space and over time? The existence of objects, concepts, and experiences can be conveyed by word or through sensory experience to blind children who do not have other disabilities. But when a child has physical or mental differences, an individual approach must be taken to make the world beyond arm's reach or memory's ability meaningful. For these children, learning will be most effective when it includes

- consistent routines that allow repetition of the same experiences with the same cues,

- expectations that are communicated clearly in a form that the child understands,

- motivating experiences and results that emphasize materials and objects that the child enjoys, and

- active participation and opportunities for communication that allow the child to experience the results of his or her own actions.

For example, a child who indicates a preferred toy or food by pointing, reaching, or gazing at it is learning that he or she can influence what happens. These basic principles will be discussed in detail in the sections that follow.

Not all additional disabilities affect a child's ability to learn or pursue an academic program. Some students with visual impairments and other disabilities may use and understand language and may learn to read and write. These children may progress in a regular academic program. However, their disabilities may still affect their participation in educational activities, and they may need special adaptations.

A visual impairment can affect students' learning and behavior in several ways, even if they do not have any learning disabilities. Physical and visual impairments that occur together may limit real experiences with places, objects, and events. Children may use restricted or repetitious language, or they may read without understanding what they are reading because they have not acquired related concepts. A child who reads about an elephant may never have seen or touched one; another child may continually talk about thunder because it is noisy and frightening. Although all children who are visually impaired may have these conceptual difficulties, children with multiple disabilities often have a limited understanding of language, which makes it especially difficult for them to absorb ideas through words and description. Connecting reading and writing to immediate experience can help to expand the child's functional literacy; the teacher of visually impaired students can offer appropriate instructional strategies in this area.

In addition, some children with visual and other impairments may be reluctant to initiate action or to take responsibility for regular tasks because these have been done for them or they have not observed others doing them. Children may seem focused on themselves and their own experiences, without interest in other people or in events taking place beyond their immediate setting. Restrictions caused by visual and physical differences may limit a child's ability to initiate and explore, and he or she may not seem curious or interested in new events. It will be essential to encourage children to try new experiences and to get information through meaningful questions in order to expand their world. For example, if someone has said, "This animal has a long tail," a child may want to ask, "Which animal?" or "What is a tail?" Asking these questions requires the child to know what is important in conversation and what questions are related to a particular topic. Suggestions for working with students with visual and multiple disabilities who are following an academic program will be discussed throughout this booklet.

BASIC TIPS

Individuals working with children with visual impairments, whether or not they have other disabilities, will find the following basic guidelines helpful in interacting with students:

- Consider the child as more like other children than different from them. Talk with the child about his or her interests and experiences and expect the child to follow rules that are appropriate to his or her developmental level.

- Always let a visually impaired child know when you are approaching or leaving. Identify yourself by name, especially if the child doesn't know you well. Never make a game of having a child guess who you are. To do so can be confusing, frightening, or frustrating to a child.

- Briefly describe aspects of the environment that might be of importance or interest to the child that he or she cannot see.

- Always ask before providing physical assistance. If the child cannot understand words, offer your hand or arm for assistance. If the child does not know you well, touch him or her only on the hands or forearms, as you might touch another person in a social situation. Reserve hugging and close physical contact for children who know you well, especially if the child is older than preschool age.

- Use words like "blind" or "visually impaired" in normal conversation with the child, but only when they are important to the topic being discussed. Feel free to use words like "look" and "see," just as you would with any other child.

- When walking with a child, encourage him or her to hold your arm near or above the elbow and to use a cane, if he or she has one. A young child might hold your wrist or forefinger. Discourage hand holding as a means of providing travel assistance; help the child understand that it is a way of expressing affection and is different from travel assistance.

In addition, the following guidelines will help make interactions with students with visual and multiple disabilities more consistent and appropriate. It may be helpful to share them with people who are new to the classroom, such as substitute teachers or new paraeducators. Additional information that applies to working with all students who are visually impaired can be found in the companion booklet, *When You Have a Visually Impaired Student in Your Classroom: A Guide for Teachers* (2002).

- Before touching or moving students, be sure to communicate with them so that they know you are approaching.

- If you are not sure that a student with multiple disabilities can hear you or understands when told what will happen, use *object symbols* (objects or parts of objects to represent an event, person, action, or object) or *touch cues* (physical contact, usually on the hand or arm, preceding a routine event). For example, if you are pushing a child in a wheelchair to lunch, give him a place mat or napkin to carry. If you are going to lift or move a child who does not understand language, use a consistent signal such as a tap on the back of the hand to let her know she will be moved. When using an object cue or physical signal, the instructor should use appropriate, consistent language to help the child in understanding words as communication. (See the discussions of routines in Chapter 4 and methods of communication in Chapter 5.)

- Provide students with more than one type of sensory input. For example, if you are dressing a student, touch his or her hand to the shirt while you say, "Put your hand in the sleeve." Some students have difficulty attending, and a touch cue helps them to anticipate experiences. Additional sensory information can also help students who are learning academic skills; thus, students with low vision and with learning disabilities could practice handwriting on paper with bold raised lines and benefit from both visual and tactile input.

- Give students ample time to respond after you prompt them. Many students with visual and multiple disabilities have neurological differences that make them slow to respond. If there is no response after five to ten seconds, then give only a little bit of help. For example, if a student doesn't respond to the prompt to put a hand in the sleeve of his or her shirt, position the hand in the sleeve, and push gently from the elbow, rather than puling the sleeve on the arm yourself. Students may become passive if others do things for them quickly, before there is a chance to respond themselves.

- Students with behavioral difficulties should also be given several seconds to comply with a direction before a consequence is applied. An adult who is frustrated or angry with a child may provide too many directions too quickly, and the child may become agitated, having had too little time to understand the directions.

- Show students materials or objects before these are used during routines. For example, hold a spoonful of food at an appropriate viewing distance before placing it in a child's mouth; allow exploration of a new hat before it is placed on the head. Allow a child to see or touch a new object before it is introduced into a routine, especially if the child is blind and has no information about the object. For example, touching a banana before it is peeled and cut or examining a stapler before being taught to use it will familiarize the child with the material.

- For all students with low vision, make sure to provide the appropriate visual environment. Simple, uncluttered environments with glare-free lighting are best. Students may need to be positioned in a particular way to make best use of their vision. Use high-contrast materials with uncluttered backgrounds. This is especially important for students with neurological damage, who may have difficulty noticing important objects in the environment. Making objects more visible will call their attention to them as well as make them easier to see. (See the discussion of environmental adaptations in Chapter 3.)

- Even if students do not speak, continue to speak to them. The tone of your voice and the relationship of your words to experiences will help them to associate words with experiences. When you speak, use brief comments focused on the target activity, using the same words repeatedly. If the child moves, turns, or indicates attention to your words, acknowledge the behavior as communication: "You looked at me when I said 'Lunch.' You must be really hungry!"

ROLES AND RESPONSIBILITIES OF TEAM MEMBERS

The educational team for a visually impaired student with other disabilities includes family members, professionals, paraeducators, and the student, just as it does for any other students with special needs. Team members will develop and implement educational goals for the student. Regular communication among team members is important to ensure consistency in the instructors' roles.

The following is a brief summary of the professionals who may participate in working with visually impaired students with additional disabilities, and of their roles and responsibilities:

- *Regular classroom teachers* are responsible for implementing those objectives that are part of the standard curriculum. In addition, they will work with students on objectives related to specialized skills, such as social skills or daily living skills, when these can be integrated into the standard curriculum. When the student spends most of the day in the regular classroom, the regular classroom teacher may coordinate the educational plan. When a student has visual and multiple disabilities, the classroom teacher and paraeducators will work closely with the teacher of visually impaired students to find ways in which the student can participate in classroom activities.

- *Teachers of students who are visually impaired* work with the student and with other team members, when appropriate, to implement educational goals related to visual impairment. For example, when a student with low vision needs to use vision to locate her own coat or when a blind student needs to use touch to recognize tactile symbols, a teacher of students with visual impairments may be the main instructor or may work with others in teaching the skills. These teachers will be involved in assessment, planning, and instruction to meet the needs of the student that are related to his or her visual impairment. They may work through consultation with family members and professionals, or through direct instructional activities. See "The Role of the Teacher of Students with Visual Impairments" for examples of this teacher's responsibilities.

- *Special educators* work with students on educational needs related to their disabilities, either in a resource room or within the regular class. When a child requires significant services related to special needs, the special educator may be the primary teacher who coordinates the educational plan. He or she is often the primary instructor of academic skills as well as for goals related to the student's special needs. Working closely with the teacher of visually impaired students and assigned paraeducators, the special educator will decide who will implement activities with visually impaired students (see "The Special Educator and the Teacher of Students with Visual Impairments: A Critical Partnership").

13

The Role of the Teacher of Students with Visual Impairments

Teachers of students who are visually impaired perform a variety of tasks related to the specialized needs that result from visual impairment. Their primary role is to perform assessments of a child's visual abilities; provide adapted materials, such as braille textbooks or worksheets, appropriate for the child's needs; and provide specialized instruction in skills essential to the visually impaired student's ability to grow and develop. These specialized skills include

- **Compensatory or functional academic skills,** including communication modes, such as tactile symbol systems, calendar boxes, sign language, braille, and assistive devices such as speech technology. These skills are used for functional activities appropriate to the individual's developmental level, such as communicating with others, labeling and recording information, and organizing time schedules.
- **Orientation and mobility (O&M),** including strategies for facilitating travel such as human guide techniques; use of standard and adaptive canes; recognition of cues and landmarks; movement through space by walking, creeping, or moving a wheelchair; and directing others or requesting assistance.
- **Social interaction,** including initiating and ending interaction; responding appropriately in social contexts (for example, shaking hands or turning toward others); using language to make a request, decline assistance, or communicate a need; expressing emotion and affection appropriately; and adjusting social responses according to the expressions of others.
- **Independent living,** including partial or complete participation in grooming, dressing, eating, food preparation, home maintenance, organization, basic health care, and other routine personal activities.
- **Recreational and leisure skills,** including making choices about leisure time; actively participating in physical and social recreational activities; trying new leisure activities; following rules in games and activities at an appropriate level; and maintaining safety during leisure activities.
- **Career education,** including exploring and expressing preferences about work roles; assuming work responsibili-

14

Christy Morrison

Learning independent living skills.

ties at home and school; understanding concepts of reward for work; participating in job experiences; and learning about jobs and adult work roles at a developmentally appropriate level.

- **Use of assistive technology,** including using technology to enhance the performance of functional and social activities. Appropriate technology may include the use of electronic switches, augmentative communication devices, low vision devices, computer software and peripheral devices, and braille production devices, such as braille notetakers or the Mountbatten brailler.
- **Visual efficiency,** including adapting the visual environment to enhance vision; combining vision with other senses to perform an activity in the most efficient way; wearing or using appropriate optical devices, including eyeglasses; communicating visual experiences to others; and increasing the use of visual skills such as scanning or spotting objects at a distance.

Together, these areas are referred to as the *expanded core curriculum,* since they are as fundamental to the education of students who are visually impaired as are mathematics, language arts, and science.

The essential functions carried out by teachers of students who are visually impaired include

15

- analyzing the classroom and other environments for access and safety related to a student's low vision or blindness, and communicating how best to organize the classroom and materials to others on the educational team (this sometimes overlaps with the responsibilities of the O&M instructor);
- conducting functional vision assessments that describe a child's use of vision in a variety of settings and activities, and making recommendations for educational adaptations related to vision;
- conducting learning media assessments to describe how a child uses his or her senses to learn and gather information, as a basis for identifying the primary channel—such as vision or touch—through which the child obtains information and the appropriate learning materials and literacy media (standard print, enlarged print, or braille);
- implementing instruction in specialized skills related to the child's visual impairment (for example, the use of low vision devices such as magnifiers and telescopes, use of vision in self-care tasks, or use of a tactile symbol system to label materials);
- providing in-service training and recommendations to the educational team and families regarding the student's visual impairment;
- obtaining or creating specialized materials related to the student's visual impairment (such as brailled books, high-contrast photographs for communication, or object cues to represent regular routines);
- participating in instruction in regular routines or classroom skills to encourage the use of vision or another adaptation related to visual impairment.

- *Orientation and mobility (O&M) specialists* work with the educational team to develop plans pertaining to a student's ability to relate to the environment and travel independently or otherwise move within it, and work with the student to implement those goals. They also evaluate the most efficient and independent means of travel for the student. Even a child who is not independently mobile can learn to control travel by using tactile cues, signals, and requests to participate in decisions about movement and travel. The O&M specialist may also provide in-service training and recommendations to the educational team and families.

- *Paraeducators* assist with implementation of the educational program by carrying out classroom routines with children as assigned by the teacher, by preparing individualized materials, by providing additional practice on skills as needed, by ensuring students' safety, and by facilitating social opportunities for students. The consistency and effectiveness of the paraeducator can make the difference in whether or not a child achieves established goals, and it is important that team members provide the support and information necessary to prepare paraeducators. In most cases, paraeducators are more effective when assigned to classrooms or groups than when assigned to individual students. Too much assistance may allow students to accept help for tasks that they can do themselves.

- *Related service personnel* such as occupational therapists, physical therapists, and speech therapists work with the family to integrate goals related to their areas of specialization into the student's educational program. Although they may also work directly with the student, in the classroom or in a separate setting, more consistent learning will often occur if the specialist works with the educational team to integrate specialized goals into daily routines. For example, an occupational therapist who works with the child on fine motor skills at mealtime will be teaching skills that can be applied immediately.

Each member of the educational team can serve as a resource in the area of his or her specialty. "Sources of Help" provides information about additional places to look for assistance.

The Special Educator and the Teacher of Students with Visual Impairments: A Critical Partnership

Many students who have visual impairments and multiple disabilities have classroom teachers who are special educators with backgrounds in such specializations as learning disabilities, severe and multiple disabilities, or mild special needs. The educational team will need to make some individual decisions about which person will work with the child on specific skills. Decisions can be made informally if the teacher of students with visual impairments and the special educator talk regularly and work together frequently. In other cases, each person's role will need to be described in writing, and the extent, specific times, and nature of instruction will need to be specified. This can be specified in the IEP or it can be arranged among two or more professionals who are collaborating. The following list includes a range of possible instructional arrangements that could be considered:

- Dual instruction: The teacher of students with visual impairments and special educator work with the child on a new or difficult routine, with each managing a different part of the task. For example, the special educator may verbally prompt a child who is learning to feed himself or herself, while the teacher of students with visual impairments records observations and notes on physical and visual responses.
- Direct instruction with gradual fading of the teacher of students with visual impairments involvement: The teacher of students with visual impairments can also work directly with a student or provide individual support during a classroom routine, but as the routine is mastered and adaptations are provided, the teacher of students with visual impairments gradually reduces his or her involvement, perhaps observing occasionally or collecting data at intervals to provide feedback to classroom staff.
- Consultative approach: The teacher of students with visual impairments may not interact with the student directly but may instead take data or record observations. As a consultant, the teacher of students with visual impairments can provide feedback to classroom staff and help to shape a learning program adapted to the child's needs.

- Direct instruction within or outside the classroom: When a specific skill needs to be developed as a result of the student's visual impairment, the teacher of students with visual impairments will work directly with the student to instruct him in the skill. Learning such skills, such as reading braille or the use of a low vision device, almost always requires individual instruction. If a skill will eventually be used in class, instruction will probably take place in the classroom at the appropriate time. In other circumstances, however, such as when a student is easily distracted, when specialized equipment is needed, or when instruction may interrupt other activities in the classroom, the educational team may decide that instruction should take place outside of class.

Clear communication about roles will ensure that each professional's time is used efficiently and that students will benefit from each person's expertise. Teachers who understand their roles will be less likely to duplicate another professional's role or overlook components of a student's educational program.

Like all students with disabilities, children with visual and multiple disabilities need an educational program that is consistent and accessible. Most children will make regular progress and will show satisfaction in learning if their instructional program is appropriate and motivating. The sections that follow explain in more detail how to provide this type of program, offer specific suggestions for working with students with varying visual abilities, and discuss the types of accommodations, materials, and assistive technology students may require. In order to plan a program appropriate to a student's needs and abilities, however, the educator first needs to understand the student's condition and its effects on his or her capabilities.

Sources of Help

A number of sources can provide additional information about students with visual and multiple disabilities and can also indicate the availability of help and technical assistance for work with these students:

- nonprofit and government agencies that serve people with developmental disabilities
- your school district's special education office, intermediate unit, or special education service center (these agencies often employ teachers of visually impaired students)
- staff specialists or consultants at some state departments of education who work with services to visually impaired students

To obtain information on how to contact sources of assistance in your state, telephone the American Foundation for the Blind (AFB) at its help-line number, 1-800-232-5463; consult the *AFB Directory of Services for Blind and Visually Impaired Persons in the United States and Canada*; or access the organization's web site at www.afb.org.

Professional organizations that include special educators (see Appendix B for complete contact information) include:

- Council for Exceptional Children's Division on Visual Impairment or other divisions related to your students' disabilities (www.cec.sped.org)
- The Association for Education and Rehabilitation of the Blind and Visually Impaired (AER) (www.aerbvi.org)
- TASH (formerly the Association for Persons with Severe Handicaps) (www.tash.org)

The organizations and resources listed in Appendix B of this book can offer additional information and assistance.

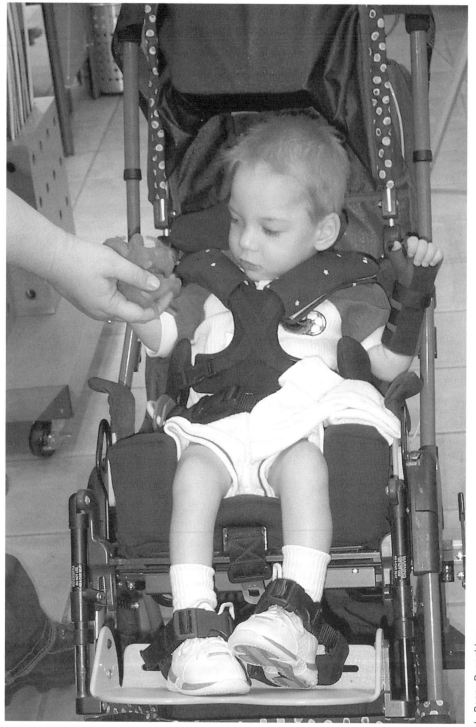

Offering interesting objects encourages children to explore their world.

2 Common Conditions among Students with Visual and Multiple Disabilities

Visual impairments can be caused by a variety of structural abnormalities and medical conditions, as well as by injury and other trauma. Many factors that cause visual impairment—most common among them premature birth, viruses and other pathologies that affect the brain, oxygen deprivation, genetic conditions, and anomalies that occur in developing fetuses—may also cause other disabilities. Because disabilities often occur together, over 50 percent of visually impaired students are estimated to have other disabling conditions (Silberman, 2000; Smith & Levack, 1997).

VISUAL CONDITIONS THAT OFTEN OCCUR WITH OTHER DISABILITIES

A number of conditions cause visual impairments. The three types of visual impairment described in this section are those that most commonly occur along with other disabilities. (See Appendix A for a list of these and other common visual impairments.) Every child is unique, but there are certain strategies and interventions that tend to work well for children with certain conditions; some of these are presented briefly. It is helpful to understand the implications of a particular condition in order to plan the best use of vision in the child's program

23

and to adapt instruction according to the child's needs. However, knowing about a given condition does not provide an exact prediction of what the child's vision will be like.

Cortical Visual Impairment

Cortical visual impairment (CVI) results from dysfunction in the systems of the brain related to vision that is caused by a developmental or traumatic brain injury. It is characterized by vision that is changeable, varying from day to day and sometimes from hour to hour, and that can be further affected by attention, perception, and alertness. Children with multiple disabilities who are alert and can concentrate on selected information will respond more readily to visual materials and events. CVI is most often caused by temporary reduction or loss of oxygen to the brain or by conditions such as cytomegalovirus or intraventricular hemorrhage that cause damage to the brain, and the level of alertness of children with CVI may vary as a result of other disabilities.

Children with this condition will often attend better in visually controlled environments and respond best to familiar objects and to environments that are free from distractions such as voices or multiple activities. They are most likely to notice moving objects, red or yellow colors, and materials placed against high-contrast backgrounds.

Strabismus

Strabismus, or muscle imbalance, is caused by damage to or dysfunction of the muscles that control the eyes. It is common in children who have cerebral palsy or other conditions that affect motor function related to the brain. A muscle imbalance causes double vision, but the brain of a young child who sees two images will repress vision in the poorer eye. This results in amblyopia—the loss of vision due to disuse. Children with this condition will rely on vision in the better eye, which may limit their ability to see on the outer edge of the visual field on the side of the poorer eye or to perceive depth accurately.

When these children are young, eye care specialists may treat the condition by "patching" the better eye (keeping it covered with an eye patch) to encourage use of vision in the poorer eye, by operations to correct the muscle imbalance, or by prescribing eyeglasses to change the angle of view. However, many children with strabismus and cerebral palsy will experience the muscle imbalance throughout their lives. Visual experiences for these children can be enhanced by

- presenting unfamiliar tasks on the side of the better eye to allow success, and presenting familiar tasks on the side of the poorer eye to challenge vision, and by

- positioning the child symmetrically as prescribed by physical and occupational therapists so that he or she can control the eye muscles.

Retinopathy of Prematurity

Retinopathy of prematurity (ROP) results from damage to the sensitive retina (inner lining) of the eye in premature infants. It can result in mild, moderate, or severe visual impairment, including total blindness. The extent of damage depends on how much the retina has separated from the main structure of the eye; vision may be reduced or lacking in the area of separation. If students with ROP have vision, they often benefit from strong, steady lighting and high contrast. Children with this condition may also have cerebral palsy, hearing impairments, mental retardation, or autism spectrum disorder related to their premature birth.

CONDITIONS THAT OCCUR WITH VISUAL IMPAIRMENT

As already indicated, many conditions frequently occur together with visual impairment, even though they may not be the cause of the visual impairment. These include certain physical disabilities, learning disabilities, mental retardation, and autism. Learning disabilities are characterized by difficulties in learning in specific skill areas when a learner has average or above average intelligence, whereas mental retardation is a general limitation in an individual's rate of and capacity for learning. When a child is also visually impaired, the effect of these conditions on learning may be significant. In addition, a combination of disabilities may cause multiple limitations that are more significant than the additive effects of the individual conditions. Some generalizations can be made about the types of interventions that are likely to be helpful for children with these conditions.

Sometimes parents and professionals assume that a visual impairment has delayed a child's development, and may overlook signs of learning difficulties that are not the result of the visual condition. Visually impaired children who do not have other disabilities do not necessarily experience global delays in reaching developmental milestones (Ferrell, 2000). If a preschooler is delayed in talking, interacting with others, exploring objects, and solving problems, an assessment should be conducted to investigate the nature and implications of the delays. Caregivers may otherwise assume that the delays are due to visual impairment alone, and may fail to consider strategies to address learning difficulties, autism spectrum disorder, or other conditions.

Physical Disabilities

Many visually impaired children also have physical disabilities due to developmental factors or injuries that affect the brain. In young children, these disabilities are often some form of cerebral palsy, although other conditions such as spina bifida or spinal cord injury sometimes occur with a visual impairment. Children with cerebral palsy often have strabismus (muscle imbalance) or retinopathy of prematurity. Optic nerve damage and cortical visual impairment may occur with spina bifida and brain or spinal cord injuries.

For these students, physical and occupational therapists are key members of the educational team. Children who do not have control of muscle systems may have limited control of eye and neck muscles that ensure that their eyes work together and that they can turn or tilt the head for best viewing. The educational team will need to consider where materials should be placed for near and distance viewing, whether special equipment is needed to support the head and trunk, and whether special positioning is necessary to allow for the best use of vision. Sometimes the team must make decisions about when to provide extra physical support; for example, a child may be provided with head support during mealtimes and when focusing on communication, but not while listening to music. This will provide the opportunity to use vision without working to support the head at some times of day and allow the child to work on head support at times when use of vision is not as important.

A blind child with a physical disability may have limited access to the physical environment. If not able to move by walking, crawling, or rolling, he or she cannot explore or manipulate materials beyond arm's reach. Therefore, objects should be placed close by to be explored; otherwise, children will need assistance to move toward what they cannot reach. They can learn from physically experiencing events and having direct contact with materials as they relate to new environments.

For example, a trip to the zoo includes opportunities to touch animals, models, and samples of food. To hear the seal barking or the noises of the wings of a hawk will provide some information about these animals, but if the child cannot touch the real animals, he or she can also learn from touching a stuffed bird or a realistic model of a seal. Contact with materials in the sequence of a routine also needs to be provided, so that the child understands how they are used during a particular process. For example, when making instant pudding a student needs to examine the box and the mix, pour the powder, touch the milk container, stir, notice that the mix is put in a bowl, and then help to serve it from the bowl. If the child completes only one step of the process, he or she will not understand how a box of powder has become pudding.

Because a child with physical disabilities and visual impairments has limited information about objects and events that are out of arm's reach, the child may pay more attention to his or her own body. He or she may not be aware that there are objects out of reach that can be interesting and entertaining, and so may resort to habits such as eye poking or rocking instead of interacting with objects and people. Caregivers should encourage interest and exploration by introducing materials that have appealing features such as sounds or textures. As the child's interest develops, more varied objects can be introduced to encourage interest and toleration of variations.

Learning Disabilities

Many students with visual impairments also have difficulties in learning. Children who were born prematurely and were affected by oxygen deprivation, or those whose parents consumed prescription medications, drugs, or alcohol, may have learning difficulties due to mild brain damage, in addition to their visual impairment. Sometimes, however, a student's learning disabilities are not identified because it is simply assumed that they are related to the visual impairment.

For these reasons, assessment is a critical step in educational programming for students with visual and multiple disabilities. Assessment of visually impaired students for the possibility of learning disabilities should involve specialists in both areas. Although many standardized tests used to assess learning disabilities can be used with students who have low vision, they should be provided in the child's primary learning medium (standard or large print, braille, or an auditory medium such as on tape). In most cases, timed tests will not be appropriate for students with this complex combination of abilities and disabilities. In addition, several tests combined with work samples and observations can provide a more complete picture of the child's abilities.

Identifying learning disabilities in a child who is blind can be especially challenging. Tests that are normally used in identifying learning disabilities are often very visual, and they are not standardized for blind learners because of the small numbers of students who read braille. Experts in learning disabilities are rarely familiar with the reading characteristics of blind children and may overemphasize the impact of blindness. Standardized tests in braille can be useful, but the psychologist or diagnostician should review the results with the teacher of visually impaired students to decide whether there is an error pattern that relates to the visual impairment or whether there are difficulties that are not typical of blind students.

Learning adaptations for students with low vision and for those with learning disabilities are often similar. High-contrast reading materials with uncluttered backgrounds, learning settings that are free of distraction, consistent routines, and predictable learning environments provide the best opportunities for success for students with combinations of visual impairment and learning disability as well as for those with either disability (see Chapter 3). The extent and type of service will depend on the child's learning difficulties, and the educational team should develop the student's Individualized Education Program (IEP) with an emphasis on compensatory skills—strategies that can enhance or replace areas of limitation affected by a disability—and environmental adaptations.

For many blind students with learning difficulties, early use of uncontracted braille may provide an opportunity to practice reading with a limited number of braille symbols. Uncontracted braille uses only the symbols for the letters of the alphabet as well as standard punctuation. Instruction in contracted braille, which includes more than 200 additional symbols, can be delayed until a child is able to decode and recognize words readily and to read fluently on grade level in uncontracted braille (see Chapter 4).

Mental Retardation

Many children with visual impairments also have mental retardation. They may learn slowly and have difficulty retaining familiar information. The visual impairment does not cause mental retardation, but both conditions may be the result of the same condition, such as Down syndrome or cytomegalovirus (CMV). When mental retardation is combined with a visual impairment, children may have particular difficulty understanding abstract concepts and relationships between events. They may not see visual cues that provide information about what is occurring or what others are feeling, and they may not be able to infer as much meaning from spoken information as students who do not have retardation.

Assessment of mental retardation is usually based on standardized assessment of intelligence along with the evaluation of adaptive skills. A teacher of visually impaired students should be involved in the assessment and should provide team members with feedback on whether or not any developmental delays are related to the visual impairment. Some visually impaired students have delays in self-care skills such as dressing, food preparation, or organization, but this does not mean that the students have retardation.

For a child with mental retardation, learning is usually most effective if instruction is consistent, involves functional routines that are repeated frequently, and includes some features that are interesting and motivating to the learner. Children with mental retardation and visual impairment are more likely to make regular learning progress when they understand the expectations and are motivated to accomplish the task. Team members must be certain to acknowledge the effects of both visual impairment and retardation in planning learning and adapting learning activities. This means that students need opportunities to practice skills in regular routines, with opportunities to practice new skills before being expected to generalize them to new situations. For example, a child who learns to put on her coat in class at the end of the school day should have regular practice with this skill before being asked to put on her coat in an unfamiliar environment, such as in a museum after a field trip. It also means that language skills should be taught in association with real experiences. Teaching materials should be concrete and functional, and reinforcement should be delivered immediately following the child's successful performance of a skill.

Autism Spectrum Disorder

Some children with visual impairments have behaviors that are characteristic of autism spectrum disorder. Difficulty in relating to or interacting with others, perseveration (repetitive behavior), echolalia (repetitive language), and rigid adherence to routine are common among blind students, particularly those with retinopathy of prematurity or other conditions that may be associated with neurological difficulties. If these behaviors are frequent and consistent, the child may be diagnosed as autistic. This diagnosis should be made by an educational team that includes specialists in both autism and visual impairment, to avoid the possibility of inappropriate diagnosis.

Providing opportunities for interaction and models of appropriate behavior can improve the child's ability to interact appropriately even if the motivation is to obtain a wanted object or event. While echolalic (repeated) language is common in young blind children, it is more common and prolonged when children have multiple disabilities. When others respond to such language as if it is an appropriate request or comment, the child will be rewarded for speaking and is more likely to make the transition to conventional language. Including a specialist in autism on the educational team may help in addressing ways to provide sufficient structure for the child to make social connections as well as to allow for the incidental learning experiences that are important for blind children.

Both children with autistic-like behaviors and those with a diagnosis of autism spectrum disorder can benefit from techniques that assist autistic children in interacting with and responding appropriately to others. Creating situations where they must initiate some behavior to be rewarded with a preferred experience may encourage interaction; for example, placing a favorite toy in an inaccessible place will make it necessary for them to request the toy, and receiving the toy will encourage them to make future requests of others. As with other conditions that cause a limited understanding of environmental interactions, the effects of autism can be modified when the environment is predictable and there are clear results of the child's behaviors.

A visual impairment can compound the effects of disabling conditions that may occur along with the visual impairment. An autistic child may be further isolated socially by blindness, for example, and a child with a learning disability may be more likely to experience conceptual confusion. For these students, precise assessment and consistent communication among team members are essential parts of an effective educational program.

Reviewing the details of an orientation and mobility lesson.

3 Educational Needs of Students Who Have Low Vision and Multiple Disabilities

Most students with multiple and visual disabilities have some vision. Therefore, it is essential, in working with such students and determining an appropriate educational program, to understand how and what they see. Families and other professionals can find out how children see by watching how they turn their heads, move their eyes, position themselves and materials they want to see, and search for objects. In addition, reviewing a student's records and obtaining appropriate assessments will produce important information.

STUDENTS WITH LOW VISION AND SEVERE MULTIPLE DISABILITIES

Use of vision can be affected by physical conditions in areas other than the eye and the optic nerve. This is especially true when there is damage to the brain, because many parts of the brain play a part in interpreting visual information. Differences in brain structure may make it difficult for a child to distinguish meaningful objects in an environment, to select visual information against a background, to interpret nonverbal cues from others, to perceive features such as depth and position in space, or to identify partial or overlapping images. Children with short memory spans may not recognize familiar objects or may not associate objects that are related to each other, such as toothpaste and a toothbrush.

Physical limitations like those caused by cerebral palsy may restrict a child's ability to interact with objects or to move toward objects of interest. That child may not attend to objects at a distance because they are not attainable; others may assume that this results from a lack of adequate distance acuity. Children with learning disabilities may appear to have visual difficulties when reading, which they may describe as double vision, letters that are difficult to read, or images that move on the page.

Assessment of Vision

Because it may be difficult to distinguish the effects of other disabilities from those of visual impairment, it is especially important for these children to receive a clinical low vision evaluation—an assessment by an optometrist or ophthalmologist with expertise in low vision—followed by an educational assessment by a team that includes specialists in visual impairment and in learning disabilities. Information from these assessments will help the team to decide what educational services the child needs. These students also need periodic reassessments of their vision.

It is difficult for an eye specialist to get specific information about a student's vision through a clinical examination if the child cannot clearly describe what he or she sees or respond to traditional measures of visual acuity (sharpness of vision) like the Snellen chart (the commonly used eye chart that evaluates acuity through identification of selected letters of the alphabet or of the position of rotated Es presented from a distance of 20 feet). Therefore, children with low vision and other disabilities need to have their vision evaluated by eye care specialists experienced in conducting low vision evaluations.

There are several assessment procedures that can be helpful in identifying the visual abilities of a child who does not respond to standard measures of vision. These procedures can be conducted by a teacher of visually impaired students with input from the classroom teacher, paraeducator, or parent. It may be particularly important to administer the test collaboratively when the specialist in visual impairment does not have daily contact with the child, so that someone is involved who understands the learner's physical abilities, communication modes, and behavioral characteristics.

Most often, the teacher of students who are visually impaired will conduct two assessments that are required in some states or districts for students to be eligible for educational services as visually impaired. A *functional vision assessment* describes a student's use of vision in typical settings. This assessment provides recommendations for how to encourage appropriate use of vision in learning. A *learning media assessment* is conducted to identify the most efficient learning medium for a student. For academic students, it will also provide information to help the team decide on whether the student will read braille, enlarged print, or standard print with or without optical devices.

Even though structured assessment can provide information about the child's visual abilities, the observations of family and the regular educational staff are critical in determining what the child can see. Fluctuations in vision throughout the day, selective visual attention to specific colors or to movement, and preferences for viewing materials from a particular position or distance are common in students who have low vision and other disabilities. Recording unusual visual behaviors or responses is important to assist specialists in determining the extent and quality of vision. Many children with visual and multiple disabilities display variations in vision, and their most efficient vision may differ from their typical vision. For example, a child who does not seem to notice his or her plate at mealtime may be fascinated with a bit of lint on the carpet ten feet away; this suggests that he or she has the optical ability to notice the small object and also that visual behaviors are affected by perception, attention, and motivation. Only individuals who are regularly in contact with a child can accurately describe variations in vision and behavior that will help to determine how much vision the child has and how that vision can be used in education.

Visual Efficiency

Visual efficiency refers to the use of vision along with other senses to complete a task quickly and effectively. The decision about whether to encourage the use of vision should be made by the educational team, based on the team's assessment, including the functional vision assessment and the learning media assessment. For a child with low vision and multiple disabilities, vision is most often used in carrying out daily routines. Such routines may include daily living skills, organization of materials, travel on familiar routes, social routines, and academic tasks when appropriate. In most cases, the use of vision should be encouraged during the routine at the time when the routine usually takes place. If there is evidence that the child can see the elements of the activity but is not regularly using vision to locate objects, manipulate materials, and ensure his or her own safety, the environmental adaptations described in the next section may encourage more frequent use of vision.

Families and teachers often ask about the usefulness of programs that increase a child's use of vision. Some children demonstrate mild improvement in vision through *vision therapy* conducted by an optometrist, but this is mainly true when their impairment is associated with a muscle imbalance or a difference in vision between the two eyes. The procedure involves activities that "exercise" the eye muscles and emphasize the use of both eyes. This requires understanding and cooperation by the participant, who must practice the exercises regularly, and thus is not appropriate for all students. Vision therapy is not an educational procedure, and should not be conducted by a teacher of visually impaired students or other educational personnel. Professionals who are asked by parents to recommend or perform vision therapy should refer the family to their eye care specialist.

The term *vision stimulation* has been used to describe methods of encouraging students to use vision. These have sometimes been interpreted as passive stimulation of vision through presentation of bright and vivid visual materials. This approach rarely results in measurable change in the use of vision, and it is viable only for infants whose brains are just developing, for people recovering from recent head injuries, and for individuals with severe physical disabilities who have few discernible movements for interacting with the environment. Professionals should be aware that passive display of visual stimuli will do little to improve the use of vision; flashing lights and shiny objects may attract attention, but they do not result in sustained learning.

The terms *vision enhancement* or *vision usage* are more appropriate than vision stimulation because they imply that the child is actively involved. Instructors can prompt the use of vision in regular tasks; enhance visual features by adding color, contrast, and other adaptations; and reinforce the child's use of vision to accomplish a task. The strategies described in the following section provide detail about encouraging vision use.

Environmental Adaptations
Modifying the environment can be an essential part of helping some students to be comfortable in the classroom,

to perceive objects and activities around them, and to obtain information for learning. Reducing background clutter, using high contrast, and marking critical objects or features with visual highlighting such as brightly colored or reflective materials are examples of adaptations that improve the visual environment for students. Using intensive lighting on the task may also attract the child's attention to important visual information. For example, a child with cortical visual impairment who does not use vision in locating a cup can sometimes be encouraged by the use of a bright red or yellow cup or by reducing room lights and using overhead light to feature the appropriate place at the table. "Environmental Adaptations to Enhance Visibility" provides details on the types of adaptations that may be considered.

Instruction by Prompting and Reinforcement

Some visually impaired students use touch to accomplish tasks that could be accomplished more efficiently with vision. They may need to relearn routines using vision, in response to prompting. Goetz and Gee (1987) suggest the following prompts to encourage students to use vision in the performance of tasks:

- Visual prompts, such as pointing toward an object or moving the object to catch the child's attention.

- Auditory prompts, including generating a sound with the object to be viewed (for example, tapping a spoon on the table) or prompting a child verbally ("Jennifer, look at the spoon.") The spoken prompt is only effective if the child clearly understands spoken language; otherwise, he or she may look at the speaker rather than at the object.

- Time-out technique, which consists of removing the object quickly when the child looks away. When the child feels for the object and does not find it, he or she

Environmental Adaptations to Enhance Visibility

A number of simple changes to the classroom environment can dramatically enhance students' abilities to obtain information, be comfortable, and engage in learning. Principles of basic organization and appropriate contrast and lighting include the following:

- **Lighting.** Make sure classroom lighting is even and consistent. Change flickering bulbs or other sources of irregular light. Observe the natural lighting sources in rooms and notice how the lighting changes throughout the day. Reduce high-glare surfaces or seat students where glare will not obstruct vision. Check for glare sources on computer screens, and use a piece of cardboard or other opaque material as a visor extending from the top of the computer. Encourage students who are light sensitive to wear caps or sunglasses in bright lighting and out of doors. For many students, standard sunglasses will work; children with light sensitivity may benefit from light-absorptive lenses prescribed by their eye care specialist.
- **Color.** Use bright colors (red, yellow, orange) against neutral, solid backgrounds. For printed materials, use black print against a cream-colored or nonglare white background.
- **Contrast.** When combining colors, use those opposite one another on the color wheel. Use shades and colors that contrast with one another, and use neutral or contrasting backgrounds when displaying materials or framing photographs. Instructors should refrain from holding visual materials in front of them while wearing patterned clothing.
- **Space and viewing distance.** In pictures, on bulletin boards, and on shelves, separate materials with space between for easy visibility. Provide bookstands and easels to reduce the students' viewing distance. Allow students to determine their own viewing distance and to position themselves as close to materials as needed.
- **Physical positioning.** Sit or lie in the areas and positions where your students are, and observe the visual environment from their perspective. For students who have physi-

cal disabilities, position them symmetrically with back aligned, shoulders horizontal, and head in a vertical position. This will assist them in seeing the most important aspects of an activity.

---

will probably look back to the location where it was. At that point, the instructor should restore the object quickly and without comment, to reinforce the child's use of vision.

- Physical prompts, which are only used if a child needs to be shown the process of moving the head or scanning. A child should not be physically guided to force a movement that he or she does not want to make. Rather, physical guidance should be used only to demonstrate a movement or position that a child cannot perform. For example, when teaching a child with a peripheral field loss to scan, you might gently move her head from left to right to demonstrate the movement. Before touching the child, it is important to explain what you will do and why.

To be successful, prompting must be done consistently and at the lowest level needed to get the child to perform the task. For example, when prompting a child to look at his or her spoon during mealtime, tapping the spoon is less intrusive than moving the child's head with your hands. Once the child has mastered the task with the prompt, the prompt should be used intermittently and then faded completely, so that the child does not regard the prompt as an element of the task.

The child also must be rewarded for accomplishing the desired task. Ideally, the reward should be a natural consequence of the task. For example, the reward for feeding oneself is the taste and sensation of eating, and the reward for putting on a jacket is becoming warmer.

When children have limitations in reasoning and mental capacities, however, more abstract consequences may not be rewarding. Being attractively dressed or pleasing others may not be reasons to do a task; thus, preferred motivations may need to be provided during or immediately after a task. Playing the tape of a favorite song during the time a child is dressing can be an incentive to continue, as long as the tape is not played when the child is not on task. A scented lotion on the hand extended for a handshake can be motivating, whereas just the touch of another person's hand may not be rewarding for some children. Occasionally, primary rewards such as food are necessary to encourage a child to perform a task, but rewards that consider the child's individual preferences are more appropriate. Food reinforcers may encourage poor eating habits and dependence on primary rewards, whereas regard for a child's individual preferences will maintain the child's motivation and interest. When a child is visually impaired, rewards may be very different than for a sighted child. Scents and lotions, vibrating toys, interesting sounds, recordings of familiar voices, or tactilely interesting materials such as textured papers or air-filled packing materials are rewards that have been successfully used to encourage learning for visually impaired children.

ACADEMIC STUDENTS

Many students with low vision and additional disabilities will participate in a regular academic program, including activities such as reading and writing. For these children, a variety of individual adaptations may be needed. In addition to the suggestions offered in this section, teachers may find the suggestions in *When You Have a Visually Impaired Student in Your Classroom* (2002) helpful in working with these children.

Structure and Organization

Students with visual impairments should be treated like other students. Classroom rules should be applied with students who have low vision and other disabilities; additional time might be set aside at the beginning of the year to make sure the student knows and understands the rules. A written copy of the rules should be available to the student to review when needed and to identify anything that he or she did to break a rule. This helps the student to regard rules as fixed and consistent, not as the whim of the teacher or other adult.

Although the student with low vision can generally use the same organizational materials as sighted peers, including notebooks, homework pad, and folders, a plan for organizing materials will also be important. This means establishing a consistent location for storage, creating a sequence for using materials, providing visible or tangible boundaries between them, maintaining routines for labeling materials, and any other features needed to allow easy access to materials. The teacher of visually impaired students may help to find materials that are visually easy to locate and that use contrast and color cues, making access to needed items easier. In addition, special devices such as magnifiers that the student uses should be stored in a consistent and accessible place (see Chapter 7, "Special Materials Used by Students with Visual and Multiple Disabilities").

The classroom teacher may want to set aside a time each week to help the student organize materials; late on Friday afternoon or first thing Monday morning may be the most logical. Sometimes a peer or friend will be willing to help the student check to make sure materials are in order at the beginning of the school day. This will help to avoid frustration or delay in beginning the lesson.

Support for Academic Skills

In general, students with low vision and learning disabilities will benefit from enhanced visual features in their academic materials. High-contrast, uncluttered backgrounds, clear visual organization, and formats that offer visible cues, such as section titles or bold print for emphasis, will make materials easier to work with.

Informal reading assessments have become a part of the regular reading curriculum, and they are especially important when a student has low vision and other learning difficulties. These assessments, also known as informal reading inventories, can be developed by teachers based on graded reading passages or can be purchased commercially. Informal reading inventories can help to determine what types of errors the student makes and whether they are related to reading knowledge or to low vision. For example, a student who confuses words with internal vowels—such as *beat* and *boat*— may be having difficulties seeing the letters, but a student who reads *bank* as *buy* may be having difficulties with basic decoding.

As noted earlier, learning disabilities often go undiagnosed in a child with mild low vision, in part because there is a tendency to assume that reading problems are a result of the visual impairment. Although many students with low vision are slower readers than their sighted peers, visual impairment alone does not account for significant difficulties in decoding or comprehension. A teacher who works with a student with low vision who has unusual difficulty in applying reading rules or understanding text should refer the student for possible assessment by specialists in learning disabilities.

Some students with low vision and additional disabilities will need to learn alternative approaches, such as use of recorded materials or synthetic speech on computers, to assist them in reading and writing. Many of these students will have particular difficulty with handwriting, and early instruction in keyboarding will allow them to maintain legible writing as their academic requirements increase.

SOCIAL SKILLS

Students with visual and other disabilities may also need additional support in developing social skills, not only in interpreting appropriate responses to people and situations but also in finding friends who appreciate their strengths and understand their challenges. Students who are blind or have severe and multiple disabilities often receive attention from others, such as extra assistance or curiosity about braille, but students with low vision and learning difficulties may often be viewed simply as awkward and slow by others in the class. Opportunities for them to assume responsibility or share their strengths should be provided to help them to develop self-esteem. This increase in self-esteem can, in turn, increase a child's comfort and his or her motivation to interact with others, which are the foundation for effective social skills.

SUMMARY

Students with low vision and multiple disabilities are at risk for a variety of learning difficulties. Because they often cannot describe what they can see, their families, teachers, and others around them make assumptions based on the children's responses to their environment. The impact of visual impairment can be understated if other disabilities are more evident, and a child's ability to use vision effectively may not be explored if the extent of his or her vision has not been assessed. Families and teachers must take a strong role as advocates for appropriate services. Like all students with visual impairments, students with multiple disabilities, including those with low vision, will benefit from high-quality clinical and educational assessment, with appropriate vision services and adaptations to support learning.

Getting off the bus.

4 Educational Needs of Students Who Are Blind and Have Multiple Disabilities

Children who are blind have no vision, or perceive only light. Most often they obtain information about the environment and learn through the use of their other senses. Techniques and considerations in working with children who are blind are therefore different in some respects from those relating to children with low vision. There are a number of principles to keep in mind when working with blind children who have additional disabilities.

STUDENTS WHO ARE BLIND AND HAVE SEVERE MULTIPLE DISABILITIES

Blind children who have other disabilities often perceive events as a collection of separate and unrelated elements that occur randomly. This is because the visual and language cues that link events and objects may not be evident to them. For example, a girl who touches an egg may not realize that it is the source of the scrambled eggs she eats for breakfast. A boy who goes to physical therapy once a week may not remember the activities from the previous week, and may cry because he does not understand what will happen; he cannot remember the therapist or the room where therapy takes place.

Like students with low vision, blind children with severe and multiple disabilities usually learn best from noticing events in predictable routines. Routines will promote learning if they are frequent and consistent, and if they include immediate events and reinforcers. For example, the child who learns to grasp her spoon and scoop with it receives reinforcement in the form of getting food in the spoon many times each day. A child who learns to tap on the closet door to request a toy receives reinforcement by being given his favorite toy each day during playtime. Students who do not understand or use words often rely on objects and sensory experiences as ways of representing routines or the steps in routines. Through the use of familiar objects, they come to understand that events occur consistently during the day and week. These objects will become associated with routines, serving as symbols of the activity. As learning advances, the object can be presented before the activity to signal that the activity is about to occur. Objects or parts of objects can also be used to offer choices to the student. For example, the top of the cereal box and the twist tie from the bread bag can symbolize a choice between cereal and toast; the child chooses by touching one or the other. Routines for these students should involve consistency in space, time, and objects.

Consistency in Space

Children who are blind and have additional physical or mental disabilities attend to immediate space and may not understand concepts such as distance and direction. A student who does not move independently cannot explore space and must rely on others for mobility. He or she may not repeat the same routes often enough to remember the sounds and physical landmarks that make one route different from other routes. For this reason, educators should make an effort to

- identify tangible landmarks the child may touch each time in moving along that route. For example, a piece of

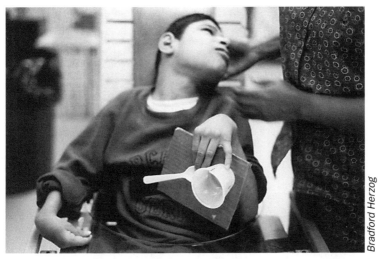

Using an object symbol to represent lunchtime.

corkboard on the wall may mark the classroom entrance, and ceramic tile may distinguish the bathroom.

- provide the child with an object or symbol that represents the destination. For example, on the way to the snack table, a place mat put in the child's lap while the wheelchair is pushed will help the child understand where he or she is going.

Consistency in Time

A child who is blind and does not understand or use spoken language has fewer cues about how events are sequenced, and does not see people doing things that signal future events—a father putting on his coat to go outside, or a mother getting out clothing in preparation for dressing him or her. It can be surprising and unpleasant when things happen without any warning, and children who cry or resist others may be reacting to not having a way of understanding what will happen next. Time can be more understandable to children in such circumstances if educators do the following:

51

- Follow a consistent daily routine in which materials can be associated with predictable activities. For example, the same cup can always be presented for snack time, and the child can be placed on the same dressing table each day when being changed.

- Use simple gestures or objects to signify the beginning or the end of an event. Thus, the sign language symbol for "finish" (hands held with palms down and moved apart) can be used, or objects associated with tasks can be put in a specific place (as in a wooden box where materials are placed when an activity is finished).

- Provide opportunities for repeated contact with objects used in functional routines. For example, using the same cup for drinking, the same cap to signal going outdoors, and the same tape recorder to begin a song will strengthen the student's understanding of the purpose of that object and the related routine. Children may not remember a routine or the function of an object if they only have contact with it once, but if they encounter it repeatedly in appropriate contexts, they will associate it with a particular experience.

- Organize a calendar box that contains objects representing activities in the daily routine (see "Using a Calendar Box for the Daily Schedule"). Encourage the child to examine items representing each new activity before the activity begins.

Objects and Materials

Objects may have a different meaning for children who have visual and multiple disabilities than they have for other individuals. When a child does not understand life routines, objects that are significant to others because they perform a function may be interesting only because of their sensory qualities. For example, a spoon is interesting because it can be used to make a noise by banging it on the table, but the

Using a Calendar Box for the Daily Schedule

For a child with a visual impairment and other disabilities, such as deaf-blindness, it can be difficult to know what events to expect each day. When a child does not have a symbolic communication system such as sign language or speech, and cannot see visual cues—such as the teacher getting out cups for snack time or a parent putting on a hat to go outdoors—experiences may seem to be random and unpredictable.

Most students will be more cooperative if they can follow a concrete schedule for their day. Calendar boxes are one way of providing this schedule. A calendar box is a long, narrow box that is separated into sections and is open at the front and top. An object that represents each major activity of the day is placed in the box. For example, a tennis shoe can represent outdoor play, and a spoon can represent lunchtime. A child can examine all the objects in the box in order at the beginning of each day and can also revisit the box before each new activity as a reminder of what will happen next. A child who has a brief memory span might carry the representative object with him or her to the activity, either in a fanny pack or on a vest with a Velcro fastener. He or she can be prompted to touch the object occasionally during the activity to associate the object with the event.

After the child associates an object with an activity, that object can also be used for communication with another person as well as for describing the daily schedule. The child may hand the object to another person to request an activity, or two objects can be placed into a slot to signal a choice of activities. As a student is able to understand more abstract symbols, a part of an object can be used instead of the entire object; for example, a shoelace can be used instead of a shoe, or the wheel of a car can be used to represent a toy car. (For more information on calendar boxes and systems see Blaha, 2001.)

child who does not hold the handle and only eats from it when fed by others is unlikely to associate it with eating.

Objects will be understood better when they are used more frequently, and new objects will need to be experienced regularly in everyday contexts before their meaning is understood. When a child does not yet understand the uses of objects, these should appear mainly in their functional role; it may confuse the child to be given a spoon for digging in the sand or a shoe as part of a musical game. In choosing materials, consider the following strategies:

- Make a list of materials such as clothing and utensils that are used in daily routines with the child. Then consider those that are used occasionally, such as rubber boots or a swimming suit. Try to determine whether the child associates the objects with events. If so, present an object before a routine to allow the child to anticipate what will happen next.

- When it is appropriate, offer two or three objects from which the child can make a choice. For example, during leisure time, present three cardboard squares with symbols attached to them. A plastic wheel to represent a truck, a Lego to stand for Lego play, and a brush used in painting will remind the student of each activity and allow him or her to select the object associated with the activity. In this way, the student is indicating his or her preferred activity.

- Note materials that are especially appealing, such as musical toys or objects that vibrate. Try to identify the characteristics that make the objects interesting, and incorporate those characteristics into objects used in regular activities. Favorite objects can also be used as a reward for completing a routine. In this case, it is important to know if the child can remember that a favorite toy will be offered after an activity is completed.

Because it is often difficult for blind children with other disabilities to understand the structure of space and time, they will usually learn the most from environments characterized by concreteness of materials and objects and possibilities for predictable interactions.

Concreteness of Materials

For the child with a limited range of concepts, learning must take place through the use of concrete, functional objects and interactive materials, not through complex or abstract materials or language. Models, abstract language, and raised-line drawings will not be meaningful to children who are still learning to associate real objects with events and to communicate preferences. Objects that are used regularly, such as clothing, tableware, and items for personal grooming, form the basis of initial learning. Classes of objects that are similar and different will not be understood until the child experiences a variety of objects in real activities.

Interactive Potential

Toys and activities that have interactive potential—that require a child to respond physically—will encourage learning. Simple cause-and-effect routines such as pressing a switch or button to start music or hitting a drum to make noise teach the child how to use movement to make something interesting happen. Similarly, getting a reaction from others by communicating also teaches the power to make things happen. Even if a child does not use words that others can understand, a response by others to that child's vocal sounds or physical movements will teach him or her that it is possible to command the attention of others.

Children who are blind and multiply disabled may be unable to initiate self-directed movement or to see objects to be attained and consequently may not be motivated to take action; therefore, they are at risk for being passive and self-involved. Opportunities for initiation and action are important, and passive activities should be kept to a minimum. While many children will prefer listening to music and being by themselves, they will more quickly learn that they have control over their environment if their voice and movements bring a response from others. Students should receive only as much assistance as needed during a task. In most cases, prompting with the voice is less controlling than touching the child or guiding his or her hand. If physical guidance is needed, the child's hand should be placed on the instructor's hand so that the child maintains control and is not physically manipulated during a task. Even if responses are limited at first, the child will learn that he or she has an effect on the world.

ACADEMIC STUDENTS WHO ARE BLIND AND HAVE OTHER DISABILITIES

Children who are blind and have other disabilities will be able to progress in an academic program, although they may need adapted instruction to do so. Children who have learning disabilities, emotional or behavioral difficulties, physical difficulties, or hearing differences may require adaptations so that they can understand and participate in instruction. For these children, specialized concerns may include structure and organization, social skills, braille, and mobility. Teachers may also consult the booklet *When You Have a Visually Impaired Student in Your Classroom* for suggestions related to teaching blind children.

Structure and Organization

Children with behavioral difficulties or learning disabilities often learn best during structured lessons where expectations are clearly stated. Having a selected list of tasks or activities can provide a child with information about goals for the lesson, and a sequence that begins with more difficult tasks and then provides choices of preferred activities can be especially successful. For example, a child may begin with a challenging writing task and reading a story, then might have a choice of several games as a third activity.

Materials should be organized in advance, and the child should be helped to arrange his or her own organizational materials early in the school year. Some organizational issues can be especially challenging for children with learning difficulties; for example, use of an appropriately sized notebook or folder for braille papers; storage areas for devices such as the braillewriter, technology materials, and cane; or procedures for turning in homework.

Social Skills

Children who are blind and have other disabilities may be at an additional disadvantage socially because they do not have information about other people's nonverbal communication, and they may not understand nuances of spoken language that reveal emotion, attitude, and intention. For example, they may not understand that a person who turns away during a conversation and gives briefer answers may want to end the conversation. They may talk too much in an effort to keep the conversation going, or they may talk only about topics that interest them. Although conversational subtleties may pose a challenge for many children who are blind, students with other disabilities may have a limited ability to integrate other cues that can compensate for the absence of vision.

These students may benefit from opportunities to listen to and talk about conversations and how they take place. The teacher may need to point out that a particular topic is being discussed or may need to point out cues that will help the child understand other people's intentions; for example, "Jack, I noticed that Denise just answered your questions but didn't say anything else to continue the conversation. When people act like that it sometimes means that they want to stop talking with you because they have something else to do."

Braille

Students who are blind and have learning disabilities or physical disabilities are often able to use braille to read, frequently with individual adaptations. (See "The Braille Code" for more information about braille.) For students who have physical difficulties such as cerebral palsy or limited use of one hand, the teacher of visually impaired students may recommend specialized adaptations for writing braille, such as the use of a one-handed braillewriter or extended keys that reduce the pressure needed to operate the braillewriter. They also may need assistance in stabilizing writing and reading materials, by clamping a book to the desk, for example, or taping down a braille paper to read. A physical or occupational therapist can recommend ways of positioning a student and his or her materials for most efficient reading.

When students have learning disabilities, a specialist in learning disabilities should be involved to make recommendations about instructional processes. These students often learn best with a program that emphasizes phonetic rules and limits the amount of new material introduced in each lesson. The use of uncontracted braille may be considered for students with learning disabilities so that they can develop strong skills in decoding without the need to memorize the large number of braille contractions. These contractions can be introduced later, after the reading process has been mastered.

Mobility

Some blind students with other disabilities have difficulty in generalizing concepts and in grasping concepts that relate to remembering directions. For example, the use of left and right or of compass directions may be particular-

The Braille Code

Children who are blind learn to read using braille. Braille is a tactile reading system based on raised dots that are formed in "cells" made up of six dots. The 26 letters of the alphabet are represented by combinations of those six dots. In addition, many words, as well as common parts of words, are represented by additional signs called *contractions*. These contractions help to save space and, in some cases, help to increase reading speed; however, they also add to the complexity of the code for new braille learners.

a	b	c	d	e	f	g

h	i	j	k	l	m	n

o	p	q	r	s	t	u

v	w	x	y	z

and	of	the	for	with

Many students with multiple disabilities use braille. Some use the entire literary braille code, which includes all contractions, while others find that the alphabet letters will meet their needs for functional reading. A blind student who has the cognitive ability to associate abstract symbols with events or experience should be assessed for the possible use of braille.

ly difficult. These students may need to learn familiar routes by sequence and memory initially; additional time will need to be spent on generalizing concepts before a child can become an independent traveler. Sometimes physical cues can provide an extra reminder; for example, a watch always worn on the left wrist can remind the student that that is the left side.

Students with physical disabilities may use wheelchairs, walkers, or crutches to travel. The collaboration of the physical therapist and the orientation and mobility (O&M) instructor can help in identifying the most practical and efficient ways of traveling. There may be times that a child may need to sacrifice independence for efficiency, as in using a wheelchair to travel between classes despite being able to walk using crutches in the classroom. This student needs to understand the options for travel and should be able to participate in decisions about types of assistance and modes of travel.

SUMMARY

Students who are blind and have multiple disabilities may have greater difficulties in integrating information and processes than other children who are blind. For this reason, these students learn best through functional and predictable routines that link concepts and procedures with real objects and tangible cues. Consistent routines will provide the foundation for more complex learning that involves new materials and experiences.

There are many types of communication systems.

5 Educational Needs of Students Who Are Deaf-Blind

A student who has both a vision and a hearing loss that require educational programming beyond what is needed for only one sensory impairment is considered to be deaf-blind. Students classified as deaf-blind often have some vision, hearing, or both. For them, the limitations of vision and communication input can diminish the information they gain about the world and restrict their development and understanding of concepts and their ability to interact with others.

Many students who are deaf-blind also have other disabilities, including retardation, autism spectrum disorder, or physical disabilities. Strategies already described for working with students with multiple disabilities, especially students who are blind, are also appropriate for many deaf-blind students: the use of objects and signals to symbolize a coming event, consistency in scheduling and activities, and communicating with the child before a transition or change in activities or events are especially necessary when a child is both deaf and blind.

ASSESSMENT

Many students with deaf-blindness have highly individualized forms of communication that may include combinations of sign language, verbal communication, pictures, objects, or symbols. The assessment team therefore needs to include members who are familiar with both vision and hearing impairment as well as someone who interacts regularly with the child. Few standardized assessments are appropriate for children with deaf-blindness, although some instruments such as the Callier-Azusa Scale (Stillman, 1978) provide a profile that is based on individual behaviors that reflect general development. Because others may not easily understand the communication of a child who is deaf-blind, there is a risk of underestimating the child's abilities. Assessments should include observation of regular routines carried out with familiar people, to demonstrate the child's ability to anticipate, make choices, request, and use expressive modes of communication to control events.

When identifying the most appropriate forms of communication for a child, team members need to consider the amount of vision and hearing available to him or her. *Receptive communication*, the understanding of the expressions of others, and *expressive communication*, the ability to express one's own thoughts and ideas, may require variations based on a child's deaf-blindness. For example, a deaf-blind child may receive communication through the presentation of materials in the environment, but will express ideas through natural gestures and selecting objects to express desires.

COMMUNICATION SYSTEMS

A number of different communication systems can be used for expressive and receptive communication with students who are deaf-blind, including American Sign Language, tactile written systems, nonsymbolic communication, picture systems, total communication, and braille. Often, a combination of systems is used, and they may be augmented by a variety of assistive devices such as Intellikeys or switches. Assistive devices can easily be adapted for children who are blind or have low vision. Adding tactile symbols, object cues, or braille can make a device accessible for a blind child; color and contrast

64

**An instructor signing close
to a visually impaired student.**

enhancements and the use of realistic pictures or photo-graphs may make a device more usable for a child with low vision.

American Sign Language

American Sign Language may be expressed or signed into the hand of the deaf-blind child who does not have enough vision to see hand shapes. People with low vision may prefer a slightly closer viewing distance than typical signers. Those who have conditions such as Usher's syndrome, in which retinitis pigmentosa decreases the visual field, may prefer an increased viewing distance so that they can see the entire sign within their visual field.

Tactile Written Systems

Tactile written systems such as braille or the Fishburne alphabet (which uses raised tactile alphabet symbols) can be used for communication by deaf-blind students who have well-developed language and can understand language structure. Braille requires more tactile discrimination ability, but almost any information can be obtained in braille, whereas Fishburne is used only for functional purposes such as labeling. Because Fishburne is large and difficult to reproduce in quantity, it is mainly useful for brief reading and writing tasks. Although it is generally used by adults, it might also be considered for children who understand letter symbols but have difficulty with tactile discrimination. The tactile symbols can be paired with printed symbols so that the deaf-blind child can receive information from print readers, who spell words by placing the child's finger on the corresponding tactile letters.

Nonsymbolic Communication

Nonsymbolic communication will be appropriate for students who cannot associate a symbol (manual sign or abstract tactile shape) with a concept. Students who use only nonsymbolic communication will receive information through the repetition of daily routines and the consistent association of objects with these routines. After they connect the object with a purpose or experience, they may learn to request and make choices from among real objects and, later, from among representations or parts of these objects. Examples of nonsymbolic communication are touch, object, and sound cues before an event; use of body contact such as hugs or hand holding; and visual communication such as smiling or waving.

Picture Systems

Picture systems are appropriate for students with low vision. These systems are organized arrays of pictures that represent common ideas for communication, such as objects, actions, descriptors, emotions, places, and other classes of words that are important for basic communication. They can be displayed individually, placed on a

Using a picture to ask for a digging spoon.

background or strip for sequencing, or added to an electronic communication device such as a switch or an augmentative speech device for automatic activation.

Existing commercial picture systems can be used, or nonstandard systems can be developed for individual students, based on their abilities and interests. When deciding on an appropriate picture system, the team should consider the student's visual ability and the importance of visual adaptations to improve visibility of

Natalie Isaak Knott

An augmentative communication device.

pictures. Simple, realistic drawings that include color are usually the most visible, and some students who have difficulty with abstract representation do best with photographs of real objects. Most students with low vision do not benefit from pictures that are larger than about three inches square.

Total Communication

Total communication is a combination of spoken and signed communication that will involve individual adaptations for the deaf-blind student to amplify sound and to allow for tactile reception of signs, if necessary.

Braille

Braille is occasionally used by deaf-blind individuals as a form of communicating, usually by means of a device such as the Tellatouch that has a keyboard for the use of the sighted person and a braille display for the blind individual. The sighted person types to converse with the deaf-blind person, who receives the words in braille and responds by typing or brailling. The response is displayed on a small screen for the sighted individual.

SUMMARY

Virtually any combination of expressive and receptive communication can be activated by technology to meet the varied communication needs of deaf-blind children. This can easily be done by attaching the appropriate input and output devices to a standard computer. Students can input their communications via a keyboard, voice, or even sign language; they can receive output through braille, speech, or print. The keys to the effective use of technology, however, are a precise assessment that identifies the individual's most efficient options for communication and the use of the communication device for functional purposes.

Some children need to be encouraged to move.

6 Behavioral Issues and Students with Visual and Multiple Disabilities

Behavior often communicates a message. Some children with sensory or other disabilities may develop their own ways of gaining attention or interacting with others that are not always recognized as attempts to communicate. It is therefore important to determine if any given behavior represents a student's wish to convey a message and to examine the child's patterns of behavior over time.

Some children with visual and multiple disabilities may display behaviors that are different from those of other children their age. Not all behaviors are necessarily communicative, and these behaviors may occur for several reasons:

- The child may be unaware of how others act because vision and hearing impairments prevent him or her from observing their behaviors.

- The child may not know how to interact with toys and materials, and may focus on his or her own body as a source of entertainment.

- The child may have neurological damage that causes him or her to enjoy unusual types and levels of sensory stimulation (such as gazing into lights or creating pain).

- The child may not have a way of letting others know about his or her wants and needs, and may behave inappropriately to communicate or express emotion.

The ways of guiding children with visual and multiple disabilities toward appropriate or desirable behaviors are not different from methods used with other children. To change a behavior, adults must first identify the precipitating factors. Often a change can be made by altering the environment or events preceding the behavior.

Sometimes unusual behaviors of children with visual and multiple disabilities are caused by physical differences: a child who has pain or discomfort may not sleep enough, or a child with brain damage may have repeated perseverative behaviors such as severe hand biting, or an aversion to being touched. Any behaviors that involve intense physical responses that interfere with the child's quality of life should be reviewed by a physician to determine whether medications may benefit the child. Families or professionals need to document the duration, intensity, and context of behaviors they would like to change. If the behavior does not occur regularly, the family may want to take a videotape of the child for a specialist to view.

To determine the reason for a behavior, specific observation and documentation are essential. The ABC method (antecedent/behavior/consequence) is a basic strategy for examining patterns and relationships in behaviors (Cartwright, Cartwright, & Ward, 1989). In this approach, when a child begins the behavior that is prompting concern (such as having tantrums, throwing materials, or engaging in body rocking), the teacher makes a note of what the behavior is and what was happening or had happened when it began, then records the result of the child's behavior: Was he or she sent to a time-out room? Did someone approach and try to soothe the child?

After several weeks of documentation, the teacher may begin to see patterns. One child may eye-poke more after awakening, or just before bed in the evening. Another child may misbehave more in the presence of a paraeducator who after a tantrum comes over and hugs the child. When such a pattern is recognized, the educational team can ask that this kind of positive reinforcement stop. Often team members will find that a behavior is being reinforced by something different from what they had thought. Adults may believe that reprimands will discourage unwanted behaviors, but the attention that children get from reprimands can be satisfying and may lead them to continue the original behavior.

STEREOTYPIC BEHAVIORS

Stereotypic behaviors (formerly called *blindisms* or *blind mannerisms*) are often a concern when a child has multiple disabilities. Because many children with retardation are not concerned with pleasing others, they may not refrain from eye poking or rocking just because someone asks them to, or because they are told they look nicer when they don't rock. These behaviors may occur because children want more stimulation or physical activity, because neurological states compel them to crave a particular type of stimulation, or because they are unaware of repetitive behaviors that are socially unacceptable.

When a child is blind or visually impaired, some types of stereotypic behaviors are especially common. Eye poking, rocking, head slapping, hand flapping, light gazing, and finger flicking at light are among those behaviors displayed by some children with visual impairments.

How to change stereotypic behavior depends to some degree on its impact on the child's life:

- Does it cause injury to the child or to others?

- Does it harm materials or the environment?

- Does it interfere with the child's ability to participate in activities?

- Does it cause social stigma because it is unattractive to others?

Educational teams who want to limit or eliminate these behaviors might consider the following strategies:

- Redirect the child to another activity that interferes with continuing the stereotypic behavior; for example, a child who engages in eye poking may be given clay or a favorite toy to play with instead.

- Reward the child for times when he or she is not engaging in the behavior; for example, a child who frequently rocks would be allowed to hear a favorite CD if he has not rocked during group time.

- Remind the child with a "secret" signal, such as a clap or whistle, that he or she is engaging in the unwanted behavior.

- Identify a specific time and place during which the child can engage in the behavior—for example, rocking in a rocking chair at free time.

LANGUAGE AND SOUND PRODUCTION

Language and sound production by many children with visual and multiple disabilities is often not meaningful or connected with reality. Sometimes these children use *echolalia*, which is repeated language that reflects a student's limited capacity for self-expression. Sometimes echolalia is meaningful for the child, as when he or she repeats "Do you want a cookie?" after the teacher has asked that question. If the child puts out a hand and shows evidence that he or she does want a cookie, responding as if he or she has made an appropriate request will help to reinforce the use of words. (Asking the child to repeat the request appropriately usually does not work, unless he or she generally uses language appropriately. Requesting that the child repeat the teacher's own words may reinforce the

74

tendency to repeat, and correcting the child will make spontaneous use of speech less likely.)

Other children speak to themselves or use words that sound like nonsense to others. This may occur because a blind child with other disabilities uses sound as a source of entertainment, out of limited understanding of how conversation relates to real events and experiences. Some of this behavior may be reduced by engaging the child in more interaction and emphasizing words that relate to events and objects within his or her immediate experience.

PASSIVITY AND LIMITED MOVEMENT

Passivity and limited movement are common when children do not have incentive to explore and cannot hold in memory the materials that are in their world. Children may sit in one place and finger the edge of their clothes rather than reaching out to discover things close at hand; when their name is called they may not crawl toward the sound even though it is recognizable. Reluctance to move is probably a result of not knowing what is there to be explored, and of not being required to move in order to enjoy experiences such as food or a favorite activity. Movement requires effort and strength, and a child who is not curious or is uncomfortable will not make that effort. Requiring children to move to achieve wanted events or objects, and allowing them to connect movement with the experience of rewards may encourage initiative. For example, a child who is going to the table for lunch may be prompted by the odor of the food and reminded that on reaching the table, he or she can eat.

At very early levels of cognitive development, children may not move because they do not understand that they can have an effect on the world. To learn this, they must have the opportunity to interact with materials that provide rewarding results of their actions. Rocking a child after he or she makes a voice sound or ringing bells when the child taps them are examples of simple rewards that will help the child understand that something pleasant happens when he or she acts.

One strategy that has been successful in facilitating cause-and-effect learning is Nielsen's Little Room, an enclosed frame in which small toys or objects are suspended close to the child (Nielsen, 1991). Objects that have interesting sensory characteristics, such as bells or containers of sachet, are available for manipulation and exploration, and the child learns to create a satisfying result by moving the object. The child explores independently, without external structure or prompting. Many children will increase the frequency and intensify the focus of their movements when they discover that they can make a pleasant sound or see moving colors by touching preferred objects.

A child who does not understand cause-and-effect responses will learn them only if the results of actions are immediate, consistent, and desirable. Some children do not have enough memory to wait even a few seconds for a desired outcome, and they may not connect their action with the result when it occurs. Therefore, the result must occur immediately when the desired behavior begins. The learner must have many opportunities to experience the results—ideally, several times a day. And the results must be desirable: if music is the reward for vocalizing, a child who does not enjoy music may not continue to vocalize. As the child begins to understand that he or she has caused something, the time between action and result can be extended, and opportunities can be generalized. For example, a child who is reluctant to walk down the hall may be encouraged by hearing music while walking. Gradually, the music can be delayed until after the child has completed longer and longer sections of the route.

Eventually, a short musical prompt can be used to encourage and then reward walking in other settings.

Specialists in orientation and mobility (O&M) can suggest ways of adapting environments and adding incentives to encourage a child to increase movement, and O&M services should be considered for all children with visual impairments, even those who are not independently mobile. Some children do not have a long enough memory span to recall what they are moving toward, and the team may consider establishing a reward that occurs along with movement. Thus, as long as the child is walking, the instructor may play recorded music that he or she enjoys; as soon as the walking stops, however, so does the music. The child will soon associate his or her own movement with music, and may begin to walk more.

Many of the unusual behaviors displayed by visually impaired students are not different from those of some students with severe retardation or autism spectrum disorder. However, they may manifest themselves differently, focusing on the child's own body and on sound play, because visual impairment limits the child's understanding of events at any distance. A behavior management approach, which applies precise rewards for positive behaviors and punishments such as loss of privileges for unwanted behaviors, can be effective. However, the team should also consider the causes of the behavior and make an effort to create a context that provides routines, experiences, and interactions that will help the child move beyond a focus on himself or herself.

**Communicating with manual signs
and augmentative speech devices.**

7 Special Materials Used by Students with Visual and Multiple Disabilities

Children with visual impairments and multiple disabilities may require a number of specialized materials as well as adaptations for learning; appropriate special materials need to be chosen on the basis of the child's abilities and needs. The following sections describe some of the materials and devices that are used particularly by children with visual and multiple impairments.

REAL OBJECTS

The earliest learning materials for students who are visually impaired and multiply disabled are functional objects and materials used in everyday routines. Cups, shoes, books, towels, ankle braces, and swimsuits can easily become associated with particular routines and give the child the chance to anticipate events. Some other objects and materials are not as familiar or as frequently used, but are also valuable in teaching about events and experiences beyond the child's immediate world. A lemon, roller skates, a turtle, or a birthday present will not be encountered as often as objects used every day but can help the child understand the world beyond his or her immediate reach.

When the child is beginning to understand sequence and routine, a *calendar box* containing real objects or parts of objects can be used to represent the daily routine. As explained in Chapter 4, each object in the calendar box represents an event in the daily routine, such as a napkin for snack time and a zipper (representing a coat) for the time when children prepare to go home. (See "Using a Calendar Box for the Daily Schedule" in Chapter 4 for more details.) Over time, pictures or tactile symbols can replace the real objects, but this happens only after the child shows understanding of the relationship between the real object and the event in which it is used. Objects as symbols form the first level of understanding language, and children often move beyond this to use symbols, words, or signs for a concept that was first represented by real objects.

OPTICAL DEVICES

Children with low vision and multiple disabilities can often benefit from the use of low vision devices such as eyeglasses, magnifiers, and telescopes to enhance their visual efficiency. Such devices, which need to be prescribed, have different functions. For example:

- Eyeglasses improve vision by the use of lenses. Tinted lenses may also reduce glare or excess light.

- Magnifiers make objects appear larger by increasing the size of the image that reaches the eye.

- Telescopes are used to enlarge the image of objects viewed at a distance.

Because it is difficult to accurately evaluate the vision of a child who does not communicate by traditional means, eye specialists experienced in working with multiply disabled people should be involved in the evaluation, and, if possible, examinations should involve more than one visit as well as direct observation of the student in typical activities. An eye specialist who relies only on medical examination and standardized screening may

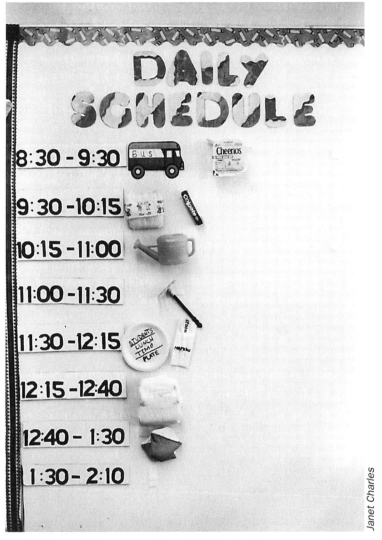

DAILY
SCHEDULE

8:30 - 9:30

9:30 - 10:15

10:15 - 11:00

11:00 - 11:30

11:30 - 12:15

12:15 - 12:40

12:40 - 1:30

1:30 - 2:10

Janet Charles

**Using pictures and real objects to represent
a daily routine.**

not gain enough information to recommend appropriate devices if the student cannot use language to respond to questions or identify symbols.

Many students with multiple disabilities use spectacle-mounted lenses because they may have physical difficulty focusing telescopes or maintaining handheld magnifiers at an appropriate distance. If they are candidates for magnifiers, stand magnifiers may be easier for them to manipulate because these devices are mounted in a frame that sits on the table. The child slides the magnifier along the material to be viewed, but does not need to hold it at a specific distance.

Children with multiple disabilities often need careful instruction to use devices efficiently. This may be true even for eyeglasses. Many children resist eyeglasses when they are introduced because the lenses change the appearance of the world, and the frames may feel unfamiliar and may reduce the child's field of vision. Parents and teachers might begin by introducing the eyeglasses only at certain times of day, ideally during favorite activities when the child experiences visual improvement. Pairing the use of eyeglasses with a reinforcing activity such as reading a favorite book or going outdoors for a walk to look for specific objects can encourage the regular use of eyeglasses. Teachers need to note any changes in behaviors when eyeglasses are used so that the eye care specialist can make necessary adjustments to a prescription; because many children cannot describe their vision, the specialist may need to rely on brief observations and feedback from families and teachers to determine the appropriateness of the prescription.

NONOPTICAL MATERIALS

Students with low vision and multiple disabilities may benefit from the use of special materials to assist with viewing distance, visibility, and illumination. Some of the most commonly used materials are listed here. (Appendix C at the end of this booklet identifies sources for these and other commonly used adaptive products. It is important to consult with a teacher of students who are visually impaired to determine whether a product will be appropriate for a particular child.)

- **Bookstands** to position visual material closer to the viewer's eyes.

- **Felt-tipped markers or pens** to create a bolder line when writing. For most students, black on a nonglare white paper provides the best contrast.

- **Lamps** that will provide high-intensity lighting on visual tasks. Some students with multiple disabilities have difficulty maintaining visual attention to tasks, and lighting the materials to be read and dimming the room lights can encourage them.

- **Sun visors or hats** can help to reduce glare and control lighting for students who are photophobic (light sensitive). Many students have the greatest difficulty with outdoor lighting, and a cap may become a symbol for going outdoors because it is always put on before leaving the building.

- **Bold-line paper** to make lines more visible for handwriting.

- **Easels or whiteboards** to allow for handwriting while standing. Many children can more easily learn writing skills on large vertical surfaces, and these allow students with low vision to get close to the writing surface without leaning over. If a whiteboard is used, teachers should make sure there is no reflected light to create glare.

- **Pictures for communication and labeling** should be chosen based on the student's vision and cognitive level. Pictures that are too abstract, contain too much detail, or have poor contrast will not be suitable for many children. Photographs of real objects provide a realistic visual representation, and simple line drawings with high color contrast can be easily recognized by students with low vision who understand the symbolism of the picture. Teachers should try several different types and sizes of pictures to determine the appropriate size for individual children. For most students, pictures do not need to be larger than about three inches square. Too much enlargement will require excessive movement for viewing and will limit the child's ability to view the entire picture.

TACTILE MATERIALS

Children whose use of vision is severely limited tend to rely more on their other senses, such as touch, both to obtain information about the environment and to accomplish tasks that others might perform using vision. Many tactile products and devices are available for people with visual impairments.

- **Braille.** Many children with multiple disabilities can master braille, a reading system of raised dots configured in six-dot cells. To read using braille, a child must have a cognitive level and auditory skills similar to those needed by a sighted child who is beginning to read print, as well as good tactile discrimination.

- **The Fishburne alphabet.** A tactile system of raised lines known as the Fishburne alphabet can be used for simple reading tasks for some blind children and adults (see Chapter 5). It may be appropriate if the student can understand the components of reading, including letters and phonetic representation, but does not have the tactile discrimination to read braille.

- **Raised marks.** Adhesive-backed dots of plastic or vinyl can be obtained from vendors who sell products for people who are blind or visually impaired (see Appendix C), or they can be created with glue. They can be used to mark parts of appliances, such as washing machine dials, increments of measurement, or other items for the blind student.

- **Braille writing devices.** Varying methods are available for writing braille. These include the **braillewriter,** a six-key mechanical device similar to a typewriter. The most popular is the Perkins brailler. The **slate and stylus** is a portable, lightweight device consisting of a frame with rows of holes in the shape of braille cells that holds paper, and a stylus that pokes through the holes, creating raised braille dots. It is used most often for personal notetaking. There is also an electronic device called a braille notetaker (see the section on Assistive Technology Devices). Adapted braillewriters are available for those who have the use of only one hand or have difficulty pressing the keys of a standard braillewriter.

- **Games and leisure materials.** Many manufactures of adaptive equipment (see Appendix C) produce tactile versions of commercial games, such as playing cards and board games.

- **Independent living adaptations.** Utensils and adaptive tools for accomplishing daily living tasks can be purchased from vendors of independent living aids (see Appendix C). Examples include the liquid-level indicator, which is placed into a glass when liquid is poured and beeps when the glass is full; containers and stabilizers for various materials; and money readers.

AUDITORY MATERIALS

Devices and products equipped to produce sound are extremely useful for gaining access to information that is usually available visually.

- **Tape recorders** can be used for making notes, listening to Talking Books (audio books), and maintaining information. For students who are reluctant to speak, recording their own voices often provides an incentive to increase the frequency of speech. Tape recorders may be the main means of information storage for blind students who do not read.

- **Audible recreational equipment** includes "beeper balls" and goal locators that can provide the blind student with a sound source during a game or activity. Commercial versions of these are available from vendors of adaptive equipment, but less expensive versions can be constructed by using a radio or kitchen timer as a sound source, or by placing a bell inside a ball so that it can be heard when rolled.

- **Auditory devices** for everyday activities provide auditory feedback to blind children so that they can independently acquire information. These devices include talking watches, calculators, clocks, money identifiers, and thermometers.

ASSISTIVE TECHNOLOGY DEVICES

Assistive technology usually refers to electronic devices and computer hardware and software that are used to make the environment, and especially print information, accessible to people with visual impairments.

- **Adaptive switches** allow students who do not use symbolic language or who have diminished motor ability to activate traditional input devices. These can include a single-switch device that can turn on a fan or a tape recorder, or they can provide multiple choices depending on the cognitive level of the student.

- **Closed-circuit television (CCTV) systems** use a camera to project a magnified image, usually of printed or written materials, on a television monitor or computer screen. Materials for projection are placed beside or below the monitor. Although they are most often used to enlarge reading materials, these systems can also be used for other tasks such as picture recognition or writing.

- **Synthetic speech,** produced by computer software in combination with a speech synthesizer, can provide spoken output of what is on the computer screen. Students can receive output in the form of words, letters, or sentences.

- **Screen enlargement software** can produce an enlarged version of what is displayed on the computer screen for students who need enlargement.

- **Braille notetakers** are portable electronic devices that are used to write braille and also include certain computer functions. The braille can be saved to a computer file or output as speech or as **refreshable braille** on a tactile braille device.

Teachers who have never worked with visually impaired students have the potential to be effective educators for these students, to contribute to their growth and development, and to receive much satisfaction from doing so. The teacher who knows how the child sees, what he or she enjoys, and how he or she communicates can respond to the child's learning strengths and needs. Observing a child's behaviors and abilities is the basis of understanding what senses he or she uses to gain information. When a child has both visual and multiple disabilities, the teacher can be the key to drawing the child out beyond his or her individual world into an understanding of routines and experiences that make up the wider world of school, home, and community. Careful assessment, consistency in teaching, and clear expectations for learning will enable the child to understand a world that may seem far away but is actually well within reach.

References

Blaha, R. (2001). Calendars for students with multiple impairments including deafblindness. Austin, TX: Texas School for the Blind and Visually Impaired.

Cartwright, G. P., Cartwright, C., & Ward, M. (1989). *Educating special learners* (3rd ed.). Belmont, CA: Wadsworth.

Ferrell, K. A. (2000). Growth and development of young children. In M. C. Holbrook & A. J. Koenig (Eds.), *Foundations of education: Vol. I: History and theory of teaching children and youths with visual impairments* (pp. 111–134). New York: AFB Press.

Goetz, L., & Gee, K. (1987). Functional vision programming: A model for teaching visual behaviors in natural contexts. In L. Goetz, D. Guess, & K. Stremel-Campbell (Eds.), *Innovative program design for individuals with dual sensory impairments* (pp. 77–97). Baltimore: Paul H. Brookes.

Nielsen, L. (1991). Spatial relations in congenitally blind infants: A study. *Journal of Visual Impairment & Blindness, 85,* 11–16.

Silberman, R. (2000). Children and youths with visual impairments and other exceptionalities. In M. C. Holbrook & A. J. Koenig (Eds.), *Foundations of education: Vol. I: History and theory of teaching children and youths with visual impairments* (pp. 173–196). New York: AFB Press.

Smith, M., & Levack, N. (1997). *Teaching students with visual and multiple impairments: A resource guide.* Austin: Texas School for the Blind and Visually Impaired.

Stillman, R. (1978). *Callier-Azusa Scale*. Dallas: South Central Regional Center for Services to Deaf-Blind Children.

When you have a visually impaired student in your classroom: A guide for teachers. (2002). New York: AFB Press.

APPENDIX A
Common Visual Impairments and Syndromes

The following are some of the common causes of visual impairments. You are likely to come across some of these terms in a student's records or in discussions with other members of the educational team. Understanding the causes and symptoms of your student's visual condition will make it easier to understand his or her special needs.

Albinism. A hereditary condition resulting in reduced visual acuity and in which there is a lack of pigment in the eyes or throughout the body. It is usually accompanied by nystagmus (see Nystagmus). People with albinism are sensitive to light and sometimes wear tinted eyeglasses indoors as well as outdoors. Because glare is particularly disturbing to them, these students usually prefer to sit away from windows. Placing a piece of black construction paper on a bright or shiny desk surface is also helpful in reducing glare.

Amblyopia. Reduced vision without observable changes in the structure of the eye. For example, when there is a muscle imbalance, called strabismus, that may result in double vision (see Strabismus), the brain may suppress vision in one eye in an effort to resolve the problem. The loss of vision is often permanent. This condition is particularly significant when vision in the other eye is adversely affected by other causes.

Aniridia. A partial or complete absence of the iris, resulting in sensitivity to light and low vision. It sometimes occurs with other physical anomalies, especially Wilm's tumor (a tumor of the kidneys).

Anophthalmia (absence of eyes) or **microthalmia** (small eyes). A congenital malformation of the globe of the eye, often associated with other physical anomalies and developmental disabilities.

Astigmatism. Blurred vision caused by an irregular curvature of the eye. As a result of the irregular curvature, light rays are not sharply focused on the retina. A student with this condition may become restless or irritable when working for extended periods. The student may also tilt his or her head or change posture to maximize vision. Copying from the chalkboard or other activities that require frequent refocusing from far to near, or vice versa, may be particularly troublesome.

Cataract. A condition in which the normally transparent lens of the eye becomes cloudy or opaque. Usually a student with this condition is sensitive to light and glare and may squint to keep extraneous light from entering the eye. Students with cataracts usually have the lens removed and replaced with an artificial lens.

CHARGE syndrome. The presence of a group of characteristics that may result in visual, hearing, and developmental disabilities. The acronym CHARGE stands for *c*oloboma (defect or fissure of any part of the eye); *h*eart defects; *a*tresia of the chonae (blockage of the nasal passage); *r*etardation of growth and development; *g*enital abnormalities; and *e*ar abnormalities or loss of hearing.

Cortical visual impairment. A visual impairment caused by dysfunction in the systems of the brain related to vision, such as the visual pathway or the occipital lobes of the brain. The degree of visual impairment can vary greatly, even from day to day, and the individual may not consistently understand or interpret what the eye sees. Cortical visual impairment is common in students who have other disabilities caused by neurological dysfunction.

DeMorsier's syndrome (septo-optic hypoplasia). Degeneration of the optic nerve related to a pituitary gland disorder. Children with this condition may be blind or have a severe visual impairment. They often have a growth disorder that can be reversed by hormones, and they may have brain dysfunction or mental retardation.

Glaucoma. A condition in which pressure of the fluid inside the eye is too high. Depending on the type of glaucoma, visual loss may be gradual, sudden, or present at birth. When visual loss is gradual, it begins with decreasing peripheral vision. If medication is prescribed to control the pressure and to prevent further damage to the eye, the student with glaucoma should be encouraged to take it regularly.

Hyperopia (farsightedness). A condition that is usually caused by the eyeball's being too short from front to back, which results in farsightedness. Close objects appear out of focus to students with this condition, who may find it difficult to do work at their desks for extended periods.

Leber's congenital amaurosis. A congenital and genetic disease of the retina, characterized by blind spots and difficulty seeing colors and detail. The disease may be progressive and result in blindness, or it may be stable with some vision. It is sometimes associated with mental retardation, neurological dysfunction, and hearing impairment.

Macular degeneration. A condition resulting in reduced acuity and a blind spot in the central portion of the visual field (the macula). Students with this condition have good peripheral and movement vision but have difficulty with work that requires good detail vision, such as reading and handwriting practice. Macular degeneration is most often a disease of older adults. Most children with macular degeneration have Stargardt's disease, a hereditary condition.

Microthalmia. *See* **Anophthalmia.**

Myopia (nearsightedness). A condition usually caused by the eyeball being too long from front to back. People with this condition can see nearby objects clearly, but distant objects appear out of focus. Using a worksheet and doing other close work may be easier for these students than may copying from the chalkboard.

Nystagmus. A condition that involves small, involuntary, rapid movements of the eyeballs from side to side, in a rotary or pendular motion or in a combination of these movements. Students with this condition may lose their place frequently when reading. Placing a cutout reading window or line marker over the reading material is helpful in alleviating this problem.

Optic atrophy. Degeneration of the optic nerve causing reduced visual acuity. In general, students with this condition hold reading material close to their eyes and prefer bright light. They may also display variable visual ability throughout the day and from day to day.

Optic nerve hypoplasia. Underdevelopment of the optic nerve, which may produce a wide range of visual functioning, from normal visual acuity to no light perception.

Retinitis pigmentosa. A hereditary degeneration of the retina that begins with night blindness and produces a gradual loss of peripheral vision. Although some people with this disease lose all their vision in adulthood, many retain some central vision with normal or reduced visual acuity. Regular-print materials are generally better than are large-print materials for these students. Travel in crowds or unfamiliar areas may be difficult because persons, objects, or obstacles in the periphery of vision (on the sides, above, or below) are not seen.

Retinopathy of prematurity. A condition often found in infants with low birth weight, resulting in reduced visual acuity or total blindness. It is usually associated with other disabilities. Retinopathy of prematurity was formerly called retrolental fibroplasia and was found in premature infants who were given oxygen during incubation.

Septo-optic hypoplasia. *See* **deMorsier's syndrome.**

Strabismus. A condition in which the eyes are not simultaneously directed to the same object as a result of an imbalance of the muscles of the eyeball.

Usher syndrome. A congenital and hereditary syndrome that affects both hearing and vision. Vision loss is due to retinitis pigmentosa. The time of onset for the sensory losses varies, depending on the type of Usher syndrome, and balance may be affected.

APPENDIX B
Organizations of Interest

The most valuable resources for additional information about visual impairment that you, your student, or the student's family may need are the teacher of visually impaired students and the O&M instructor who are assigned to your school. These specialists are familiar with national and local groups dedicated to serving visually impaired students; you may consult them regarding services, referrals, or further information.

In addition, the organizations listed in this appendix are primary sources of information and referral and are a good place to start in looking for answers to any questions about visual impairment, services for people who are visually impaired, and ways to assist your student and his or her family. *The AFB Directory of Services for Blind and Visually Impaired Persons in the United States and Canada*, published by the American Foundation for the Blind, offers more comprehensive listings of organizations, services, and volunteer groups in your state and nationwide. It can also be searched online at the AFB web site, www.afb.org.

American Council of the Blind
1155 15th Street, NW, Suite 1004
Washington, DC 20005
202-467-5081 or 800-424-8666
Fax: 202-467-5085
E-mail: info@acb.org
www.acb.org

A national clearinghouse for information, the council promotes the effective participation of blind people in all aspects of society. It provides information and referral; legal assistance and representation;

scholarships; leadership and legislative training; consumer advocate support; assistance in technological research; a speaker referral service; consultative and advisory services to individuals, organizations, and agencies; and assistance with developing programs.

American Foundation for the Blind

11 Penn Plaza, Suite 300
New York, NY 10001
212-502-7600 or 800-232-5463 (800-AFB-LINE)
Fax: 212-502-7777
E-mail: afbinfo@afb.net
www.afb.org

This national organization provides services to and acts as an information clearinghouse for people who are visually impaired and their families, the public, professionals, schools, organizations, and corporations and operates a toll-free information hotline. It conducts research and mounts program initiatives to promote the inclusion of visually impaired persons, especially in the areas of literacy, technology, aging, and employment; advocates for services and legislation; and maintains the M. C. Migel Memorial Library and the Helen Keller Archives. AFB maintains offices in Atlanta; Dallas; Huntington, West Virginia; and San Francisco and a governmental relations office in Washington, DC. It produces videos and publishes books, pamphlets, the *Directory of Services for Blind and Visually Impaired Persons in the United States and Canada*, the *Journal of Visual Impairment & Blindness*, and *Access World: Technology and People with Visual Impairments*.

American Printing House for the Blind

1839 Frankfort Avenue
Louisville, KY 40206
502-895-2405 or 800-223-1839
Fax: 502-899-2274
E-mail: info@aph.org
www.aph.org

This national organization receives an annual appropriation from Congress to provide textbooks and educational aids for legally blind students who attend elementary and secondary schools or special educational institutions. It produces a wide variety of books and learning materials in braille and other media and manufactures computer-access equipment, software, and special education and reading devices for visually impaired persons. The organization maintains an educational research and development program and a reference catalog database providing information about textbooks and other materials that are produced in accessible media.

Association for Education and Rehabilitation of the Blind and Visually Impaired
4600 Duke Street, Suite 430
Alexandria, VA 22304
703-823-9690 or 877-492-2708
Fax: 703-823-9695
E-mail: aer@aerbvi.org
www.aerbvi.org

The association serves as the membership organization for professionals who work in all phases of education and rehabilitation with visually impaired persons of all ages on the local, regional, national, and international levels. It seeks to develop and promote professional excellence through such support services as continuing education, publications, information dissemination, lobbying and advocacy, and conferences and workshops.

Council for Exceptional Children Division on Visual Impairments
1110 North Glebe Road, Suite 300
Arlington, VA 22201-5704
703-620-3660 or 888-CEC-SPED; 703-264-9446 (TTY; text only)
Fax: 703-264-9494
E-mail: service@cec.sped.org
www.cec.sped.org
www.ed.arizona.edu/dvi (Division on Visual Impairments)

The council is a professional organization of teachers, school administrators, and others who are concerned with children who require special services. It publishes periodicals, books, and other materials on teaching exceptional children, advocates for appropriate government policies, provides professional development, and disseminates information on effective instructional strategies. The Division on Visual Impairments focuses on the education of children who are visually impaired and the concerns of professionals who work with them.

DB-LINK (The National Information Clearinghouse on Children Who Are Deaf-Blind)
345 North Monmouth Avenue
Monmouth, OR 97361
800-438-9376; 800-854-7013 (TTY)
www.tr.wou.edu/dblink

DB-LINK serves as a federally funded clearinghouse that provides information and copies of written materials related to infants, children, and youths who have both visual and hearing impairments. It publishes the newsletter *Deaf-Blind Perspectives.*

**Helen Keller National Center
for Deaf-Blind Youths and Adults**
111 Middle Neck Road
Sands Point, NY 11050
(516) 944-8900 (voice and TDD)
E-mail: hkncinfo@rcn.com
www.hknc.org

The Helen Keller National Center for Deaf-Blind Youths and Adults provides services and technical assistance to individuals who are deaf-blind and their families and maintains a network of regional and affiliate agencies. Its National Training Team also offers seminars, on-site conferences, and short-term programs to increase knowledge and support the development of skills specific to deaf-blindness in those working with consumers who are deaf-blind across the country.

**National Association for Parents
of Children with Visual Impairments**
P.O. Box 317
Watertown, MA 02272-0317

100

617-972-7444 or 800-562-6265
Fax: 617-972-7444
www.napvi.org

This membership association supports state and local parents' groups and conducts advocacy workshops for parents of visually impaired children and youths. In addition, it operates a national clearinghouse for information, education, and referral; fosters communication among federal, state, and local agencies that provide services or funding for services; and promotes public understanding of the needs and rights of visually impaired children and youths.

National Federation of the Blind
1800 Johnson Street
Baltimore, MD 21230
410-659-9314
Fax: 410-685-5653
E-mail: nfb@nfb.org
www.nfb.org

The federation, with affiliates in all states and the District of Columbia, works to improve the social and economic conditions of visually impaired persons. It evaluates programs and provides assistance in establishing new ones, grants scholarships to people who are visually impaired, and conducts a public education program. It also publishes *The Braille Monitor* and *Future Reflections*, a magazine for parents.

National Dissemination Center for Children with Disabilities
P.O. Box 1492
Washington, DC 20013-1492
800-695-0285 (voice/TTY/TDD)
Fax: 202-884-8441
www.nichcy.org

Formerly the National Information Center for Children and Youth with Disabilities, the center serves as a national information clearinghouse on subjects related to children and youths with disabilities. It provides information and referral to national, state, and local resources and disseminates numerous free publications.

National Organization for Rare Disorders
100 Route 37, P.O. Box 8923
New Fairfield, CT 06812-8923
203-746-6518 or 800-999-6673; 203-746-6927 (TTY/TDD)
Fax: 203-746-6481
www.rarediseases.org

The National Organization for Rare Disorders serves as an information clearinghouse on thousands of rare disorders. It brings together families with similar disorders for mutual support. It promotes research, accumulates and disseminates information about special drugs and devices, and maintains a database on rare diseases.

National Technical Assistance Consortium for Children and Young Adults Who Are Deaf-Blind
Western Oregon University Teaching Research
345 North Monmouth Avenue
Monmouth, OR 97361
503-838-8391; 503-838-8821 (TTY/TDD)
Fax: 503-838-8150
www.tr.wou.edu/ntac/

The consortium provides technical assistance to families and agencies serving children and young adults who are deaf-blind. NTAC is a federally funded consortium project of Teaching Research and the Helen Keller National Center.

TASH (formerly The Association for Persons with Severe Handicaps)
29 West Susquehanna Avenue, Suite 210
Baltimore, MD 21204
410-828-8274 or 800-482-8274; 410-828-1306 (TDD/TTY)
Fax: 410-828-6706
www.tash.org

TASH is an advocacy organization for professionals who work with infants, children, and youths who have severe disabilities and their families. TASH holds an annual national conference and publishes the *Journal of the Association for Persons with Severe Handicaps* and the *TASH Newsletter*, and has a committee on early childhood that meets at the annual conference. There are state or regional TASH chapters.

Texas School for the Blind and Visually Impaired
1100 West 45th Street
Austin, TX 78756-3494
512-454-8631 or 800-872-5273
Fax: 512-206-9452
www.tsbvi.edu

Texas School for the Blind and Visually Impaired offers on its web site considerable information and resources about visual impairment, instruction, technology, assessment, and other areas of interest, including a large section on teaching students who have visual and multiple disabilities. It also publishes and sells professional books, assessments, curricula, and videotapes.

APPENDIX C
Sources of Products and Services

The following organizations and companies provide a wide variety of specialized nonoptical products and services that are useful in working with students who are blind or visually impaired, including many that have been mentioned in this booklet. It is always important to check with a teacher of students who are visually impaired to decide whether a product will be appropriate for a particular child.

American Printing House for the Blind
1839 Frankfort Avenue
Louisville, KY 40206-0085
502-895-2405 or 800-223-1839
E-mail: info@aph.org
www.aph.org
The American Printing House for the Blind publishes braille, large-print, recorded, CD-ROM, and tactile graphic publications; manufactures a wide assortment of educational and daily living products; modifies and develops computer-access equipment and software; maintains an educational research and development program concerned with educational methods and educational aids; and provides a reference-catalog service for volunteer-produced textbooks in all media for students who are visually impaired and for information about other sources of related materials.

Exceptional Teaching Aids
20102 Woodbine Avenue
Castro Valley, CA 94546
415-582-4859 or 800-549-6999
www.exceptionalteaching.com

Exceptional Teaching Aids manufactures and distributes educational materials and equipment for visually impaired students, including tutorial and other educational software programs; braille materials for reading readiness, math readiness, and math practice; and books on cassette.

Howe Press of the Perkins School for the Blind
175 North Beacon Street
Watertown, MA 02171
617-924-3400
Fax: 617-926-2027
E-mail: HowePress@perkins.put.kas.ma.us
www.perkins.pvt.k12.ma.us/brailler.htm

Howe Press manufactures and sells a variety of products for visually impaired persons, including the Perkins brailler (manual or electric), slates, styli, mathematical aids, braille games, braille-vision books for children, heavy- and light-grade braille paper, and Tactile Drawing Kits.

Independent Living Aids
200 Robins Lane
Jericho, NY 11753
516-937-1848 or 800-537-2118
E-mail: can-do@independentliving.com
www.independentliving.com

The Independent Living Aids catalog provides a wide variety of adaptive products for individuals who are blind or visually impaired.

LS&S
P.O. Box 673
Northbrook, IL 60065
847-498-9777 or 800-468-4789; 866-317-8533 (TTY/TDD)
Fax: 847-498-1482
E-mail: info@lssproducts.com
www.lssgroup.com

LS&S offers a wide variety of products for independent living for people who are visually impaired or hearing impaired.

MaxiAids
42 Executive Boulevard
Farmingdale, NY 11735
631-752-0521 or 800-522-6294 (for orders); 800-281-3555 (TTY)
Fax: 631-752-0689
E-mail: inquiries@maxiaids.com
www.maxiaids.com

MaxiAids distributes a wide variety of adaptive products and products for independent living.

National Braille Press
88 St. Stephen Street
Boston, MA 02115
617-266-6160 or 888-965-8965
Fax: 617-437-0456
E-mail: orders@nbp.org
www.nbp.org

The National Braille Press provides braille printing services for publishers and other organizations, including the Library of Congress; offers transcription of documents related to school or work; and sponsors a children's Braille Book-of the-Month Club.

National Library Service for the Blind
and Physically Handicapped
Library of Congress
1291 Taylor Street, NW
Washington, DC 20542
202-707-5100 or 800-424-8567; 202-707-0744 (TDD)
Fax: 202-707-0712
E-mail: nls@loc.gov
www.loc.gov/nls

The National Library Service for the Blind and Physically Handicapped conducts a national program to distribute free reading materials—classics, current fiction, and general nonfiction—in braille and on recorded disks and cassettes to visually and physically handicapped persons who cannot utilize ordinary printed materials. Materials are distributed and playback equipment is lent free of charge through a network of regional and subregional libraries and machine-lending agencies. In addition, the service operates a reference information section on all aspects of blindness and other physical disabilities that affect reading. It functions as a bibliographic center on reading materials for people with disabilities and organizations that lend reading materials in special media.

Recording for the Blind and Dyslexic
20 Roszel Road
Princeton, NJ 08540
609-452-0606 or 800-883-7201
E-mail: custserv@rfbd.org
www.rfbd.org

This organization lends recorded and electronic materials and textbooks at no charge to people who cannot read standard print because of visual, physical, or learning disabilities.

APPENDIX D
Suggestions for Further Reading

Chen, D. (Ed.). (1999). *Essential elements in early intervention: Visual impairment and multiple disabilities.* New York: AFB Press.

Chen, D., & Dote-Kwan, J. (Eds.). (1995). *Starting points: Instructional practices for young children whose multiple disabilities include visual impairment.* Los Angeles: Blind Children's Center.

Downing, J. (Ed.). (1996). *Including students with severe and multiple disabilities in typical classrooms: Practical strategies for teachers.* Baltimore: Paul H. Brookes.

Ferrell, K. (1985). *Reach out and teach: Meeting the training needs of parents of visually and multiply handicapped young children.* New York: AFB Press.

Haring, N., & Romer, L. (Eds.). (1995). *Welcoming students who are deaf-blind into typical classrooms: Facilitating school participation, learning, and friendships.* Baltimore: Paul H. Brookes.

Heller, K., Alberto, P., Forney, P., & Schwartzman, M. (1996). *Understanding physical, sensory, and health impairments: Characteristics and educational implications.* Pacific Grove, CA: Brookes/Cole.

Holbrook, M. C. (Ed.). (1996). *Children with visual impairments: A parent's guide.* Bethesda, MD: Woodbine House.

Holbrook, M. C., & Koenig, A. J. (Eds.). (2000). *Foundations of education* (2nd ed). Vol. 1: *History and theory of teaching children and youths with visual impairments.* Vol. 2: *Instruc-*

tional strategies for teaching children and youths with visual impairments. New York: AFB Press.

Huebner, K., Prickett, J., Welch, T., & Joffee, E. (Eds.). (1995). *Hand in hand: Essentials of communication and orientation and mobility for young children who are deaf-blind*. New York: AFB Press.

Langley, M.B. (2001). *ISAVE: Individualized Systematic Assessment of Visual Efficiency*. Louisville: American Printing House for the Blind.

Pugh, G. S., & Erin, J. (Eds.). (1999). *Blind and visually impaired students: Educational service guidelines*. Watertown, MA: Perkins School for the Blind in cooperation with the National Association of State Directors of Special Education.

Sacks, S., & Silberman, R. (Eds.). (1998). *Educating students who have visual impairments with other disabilities*. Baltimore: Paul H. Brookes.

Smith, M., & Levack, N. (1996). *Teaching students with visual and multiple impairments: A resource guide*. Austin: Texas School for the Blind and Visually Impaired.

When you have a visually impaired student in your classroom: A guide for teachers. (2002). New York: AFB Press.

About the Contributors

Jane N. Erin, Ph.D., is Professor and Coordinator of Programs in Visual Impairment in the Department of Special Education, Rehabilitation and School Psychology at the University of Arizona, Tucson. She is the co-author of *Visual Handicaps and Learning* and the co-editor of *Diversity and Visual Impairment: The Influence of Race, Gender, Religion, and Ethnicity on the Individual,* served as editor in chief of the *Journal of Visual Impairment & Blindness* from 1998 to 2001, and is a former executive editor of *RE:view.* Her writing and research interests are in the area of education of students with visual and multiple disabilities, braille reading, and parent and family issues related to visual impairment, and she has written numerous articles, chapters, and presentations. Dr. Erin previously held presidencies of state or local chapters of the Association for Education and Rehabilitation of the Blind and Visually Impaired (AER) and the Council for Exceptional Children in Arizona and Texas, and she is the recipient of the 2000 Margaret Bluhm Award in Arizona and the 1996 Mary K. Bauman national award for contributions to education in visual impairment, both from AER.

Susan J. Spungin, Ed.D., Consulting Editor, is Vice President, International Programs and Special Projects, American Foundation for the Blind, New York, New York.